Seminary Theology
TEACHING IN A CONTEMPLATIVE WAY

Edited by Deacon James Keating, PhD

THE INSTITUTE FOR PRIESTLY FORMATION
IPF PUBLICATIONS

Contributors

Father Dennis J. Billy, CSsR, PhD, holds the John Cardinal Krol Chair in Moral Theology at Saint Charles Borromeo Seminary, Philadelphia, PA.

Perry Cahall, PhD, is Associate Professor of Theology and Church History in the School of Theology at the Pontifical College Josephinum, Columbus, OH.

John Gresham, PhD, is Associate Professor of Systematic Theology at Kenrick-Glennon Seminary, St. Louis, MO.

Deacon James Keating, PhD, is Director of Theological Formation at The Institute for Priestly Formation, Creighton University, Omaha, NE.

Father Thomas J. Lane, STD, is Assistant Professor of Sacred Scripture at Mount St. Mary's Seminary, Emmitsburg, MD.

Father Thomas McDermott, OP, STD, is Assistant Professor of Spiritual Theology and Director of Spiritual Formation at Kenrick-Glennon Seminary, St. Louis, MO.

Margaret M. Turek, STD, is Associate Professor of Systematic Theology at St. Patrick's Seminary, Menlo Park, CA.

NIHIL OBSTAT: Father Joseph C. Taphorn, JCL

IMPRIMATUR: † Most Reverend George J. Lucas
                Archbishop of Omaha
                April 26, 2010

THE INSTITUTE FOR PRIESTLY FORMATION
IPF PUBLICATIONS
2500 California Plaza
Omaha, Nebraska 68178
www.IPFpublications.com

Printed in the United States of America
ISBN-13: 978-0-9843792-0-0
ISBN-10: 0-9843792-0-7

Cover design by Timothy D. Boatright
Marketing Associates, U.S.A., Tampa, Florida

Cover photograph by Rosario Sanguedolce

The Institute for Priestly Formation
Mission Statement

The Institute for Priestly Formation was founded to assist bishops in the spiritual formation of diocesan seminarians and priests in the Roman Catholic Church. The Institute responds to the need to foster spiritual formation as the integrating and governing principle of all aspects of priestly formation. Inspired by the biblical-evangelical spirituality of Ignatius Loyola, this spiritual formation has as its goal the cultivation of a deep interior communion with Christ; from such communion the priest shares in Christ's own pastoral charity. In carrying out its mission, the Institute directly serves diocesan seminarians and priests as well as those who are responsible for diocesan priestly formation.

THE INSTITUTE FOR PRIESTLY FORMATION
Creighton University
2500 California Plaza
Omaha, Nebraska 68178
www.creighton.edu/ipf
ipf@creighton.edu

Dedication

This book is dedicated to

Most Reverend Robert J. Carlson
Archbishop of St. Louis

for his continued and generous support of the mission of
The Institute for Priestly Formation.

Table of Contents

Section 1: Vision for Renewal

Section 2: Sources of Wisdom

Section 3: Models of Writing and Teaching

Section 4: Synthesis

Foreword

Francis Cardinal George, OMI
Archbishop of Chicago

This book contains the fruit of an Academic Seminar for seminary theologians that was sponsored by The Institute for Priestly Formation and held at Creighton University in Omaha, Nebraska. The Seminar, which is an annual event, seeks to gather seminary professors from around the country to contemplate and discuss how the teaching of theology in seminaries can flow from a more spiritual, rather than simply academic, foundation. Inspired by the U.S. Bishops' *Program of Priestly Formation*, these Seminars endeavor to explore how spiritual formation can be at the heart and core of seminary academic life.[1]

The effort to explore seminary theology from a more contemplative perspective should strengthen the formation of a priesthood that is at once both spiritual and intellectual. For the Church to be true to who She is, lay people working in the world need spiritual leaders who have labored hard to understand how love for God intersects with love for truth. Such work is best accomplished under the leadership of theologians who have, themselves, labored at their desks, both interpreting texts *and* inheriting the encounter with God that these texts mediate. As Pope Benedict XVI has noted, "Knowledge of God is not enough. For a true encounter with him one must also love him. Knowledge must become love."[2]

In this book, we see theologians who truly believe that spiritual growth in seminarians is not simply a facet of seminary formation but is to be established as learning's *foundation*. Seminary theologians have a dignity and vocation all their own. They are not university professors "in exile." Their responsibility of teaching theology is ordered toward the unique goals of seminary formation. They are to assist in forming emotionally mature priests who are receptive to the gifts of the Holy Spirit, in love with the truth of Church teaching, and compelled to deepen these realities in a contemplative study that elicits pastoral desire. Pope John Paul II captured the nature of this work by seminary theologians when he taught:

> To be pastorally effective, intellectual formation is to be integrated with a spirituality marked by a personal experience of God. In this way a purely abstract approach to knowledge is overcome in favor of that intelligence of heart which knows "how to look beyond," and then is in a position to communicate the mystery of God to the people.[3]

It is my hope that this book finds its way into the hands of seminary theologians everywhere so that they may use it as a resource for faculty development. I further hope that it will be a catalyst for discussion about the role of the theologian in the formation of priests, a role that takes seriously not only intellectual competency but also spiritual communion with the Mysteries of Christ. I am grateful to the book's contributors and to its editor, Deacon James Keating. With many other bishops, I am thankful for The Institute for Priestly Formation.

Notes

1   United States Conference of Catholic Bishops, *Program of Priestly Formation*, 5th ed. (Washington, DC: USCCB, 2006), 115.

2   Pope Benedict XVI visit to Gregorian University, November 3, 2006.

3   John Paul II, *Pastores Dabo Vobis* (1992), 51.

Introduction

Deacon James Keating, PhD

Eusebius first gave the title of theologian to John the Evangelist. This title reflected John's capacity to communicate the true doctrine of Christ.[1] All theologians aspire to be true communicators, bridging the distance between what they receive in prayerful study and what they share with their students. Since the "what" received by them is also "Who," the location of this "bridge"—the theologian—can suffer this reception very deeply. Augustine describes this freely-received suffering as an "invasion of divine speech entering the soul" of the theologian.[2] Contemplative theologians, in turning to God, are not simply suffering the limits of their finite intellect when developing a class or writing a book, but they are suffering a progressively deeper indwelling of God. As Gabriel Marcel noted, "the deepest part of me is Another." Likewise, Hans Urs von Balthasar summarized all of metaphysics under the mystery of love.[3]

1

Theologians long to have the core of their being vulnerable to the coming of God in Christ.

Communion between theologians and the God they study is wrought by the purification and suffering known personally in their own intellectual, moral, affective, and religious conversion. God wants to live within them so that they can put an affectively-imbued mind, molded by love, at the service of the formation of priests. Seminary theologians ought not to be "the last enlightenment rationalists"[4] but the first of a new generation of mystic thinkers, drawing intellectual acumen from personal participation in the Paschal Mystery. They are called to enter the ascetical life in the hope of yielding a purified heart because the purified heart sees the divine light: wisdom. The pure heart possesses them and orders their theological work toward its fulfillment in prayerful discourse on the truth of who Christ is. Pope Benedict XVI expresses this reality as follows: "Faith ... is an encounter with the living God ... But it is also a purifying force for reason itself.... Faith liberates reason to do its work more effectively and to see its proper object more clearly."[5] Who are the predecessors of today's theologians? They are those men and women who became experts at receiving and suffering the arrival of a pure heart.

In the formation of the diocesan priest, the pure heart of the professor helps to order the theology the seminarian studies toward increasing pastoral desire. This desire is enflamed and then rationally ordered by a life of interiority in the context of sacramental worship. Seminary theology serves pastoral desire: It deepens it, purifies it, and orders it rightly in ways that respect the seminarian's capacity to receive the truths of Christ.

To teach with the deepening of pastoral desire in mind becomes a valuable characteristic of those who teach theology to seminarians. The authors in this collection hope to stimulate the thought and imagination of other theologians as they ponder how best to teach theology to future priests. It is the hope of those who further the mission of The Institute for Priestly Formation that teaching methods will flow from the love of contemplation, the fruit of prayer, the result of a professor's entering into *lectio divina* as the normal preparation for teaching, and the normal execution of teaching. Future priests must be intellectuals but intellectuals who truly approach doctrinal truths in love, a love that arises from encountering God in study itself. This way, the affective life, enflamed by the truth, will secure that seminarians will not close their theology books after ordination but simply continue to go to them again and again, for study is the place they encounter His love and healing.

Notes

1   Rino Fisichella and Rene Latourelle, eds. *Dictionary of Fundamental Theology* (New York: Crossroad, 2000), 1060.

2   R. R. Reno, "The Return of the Fathers," *First Things* (November 2006): 18.

3   See David L. Schindler, ed., *Love Alone Is Credible: Hans Urs Von Balthasar As Interpreter of the Catholic Tradition* (Grand Rapids, MI: Wm. B. Eerdmans Publishing, 2008).

4   Reno, 16.

5   Pope Benedict XVI, *Deus Caritas Est*, 28.

Section 1

Vision for Renewal

Regenerating Seminary Theology
Intimacy with the Mind of Christ

Deacon James Keating, PhD

Denis, in *The Divine Names*, wrote of Hierotheus that
"he is perfect not only in learning divine things,
but in suffering them as well."[1]

Thinking in Prayer

The current pattern of academic seminary teaching is too narrow a reality to truly reverence and include all that human reason includes and that seminarian formation demands. As a way of proceeding into a new model of teaching, I want to explore the principles used in some approaches to spiritual direction. I choose this methodology because of the U.S. Bishops' call to make spiritual formation the heart and core of seminary formation around which all other formational realties must be integrated (PPF 115). The Congregation for Clergy has also called for a clearer focus upon spiritual formation in seminaries. "In [seminaries], we are developing a culture of excellence, putting special emphasis on the integral formation of the person, especially his spiritual dimension, which runs the risk of being forgotten in a secularized society."[2] Other types of spiritual models could be explored using such sources as the contours of the Liturgy, the processes of *lectio divina*, and devotion to the saints. I am electing spiritual direction as a source for teaching theology because of its power to elicit a conversion, both affectively and intellectually within the context of prayer.

Intellectual conversion within a context of prayer is a real phenomenon but one not fully appreciated within the methods of seminary classroom teaching. How can we utilize the mission of spiritual direction to assist theologians in developing models of intellectual conversion incited by intimacy with Christ? Such models for teaching will broaden our concept of reason and so lead seminarians to receive a contemplative theology as the norm. This contemplative approach carries with it a deeper involvement of the affect, making ongoing study of theology after ordination a more likely reality.

What are characteristics of the current seminary academic model? This is an approach to learning that highly esteems the objective, disinterested gathering of data in the search for truth. Here, one takes a historical, philosophic, or scientific approach to the data on revelation and endeavors to articulate one's findings on such from a predominantly critical stance. This approach is divided into many branches of thought emanating from the twin sources of theology, divine revelation and reason's reflection upon faith. These branches (Scriptural studies, systematic, moral theology, etc.) are then explored in a specialized way within individual classes that meet in succession on a weekly calendar.

Along with academic study, the seminary calendar also includes Eucharistic liturgy, pastoral ministry, dining, recreation, fellowship, individual student study time, student meetings with formators and spiritual directors, faculty meetings, committee meetings, private and public devotions, and public Liturgy of the Hours. Despite the busyness of such a *horarium*, the academic component weighs most upon the seminarian's imagination and emotional life.[3] The academic carries a judgment about competency that does not obtain within the ways formators measure pastoral and spiritual competency. The entire culture at many seminaries could be called "academic" as the values of teaching permeate, orient, and order the calendar of the formation community. The weakness of such a dominant academic model is that spiritual formation as an integrating reality holds marginal influence compared to the reign of the classroom, its methods, assignments, personnel, and chronological demands. Seminary theology dominates this environment for good reason; the priest needs to become an intellectual. But within the rush of so many assignments, readings, and tests, where spirituality oftentimes is marginalized as "private," do academics, in fact, "produce" intellectuals, masters in theology? How many of our students love and read theology after ordination? Theologians attempt to form seminarians in the discipline of looking at texts from a critical point of view; what would happen to the intellect if they also created a classroom that was hospitable to communion with Christ?[4] What type of shift in seminary culture would be needed to contextualize the academic model *within spiritual formation*. Academic formators would still endeavor to teach the mysteries but from within the context of prayer, from within communion with Christ's own love of truth—the fruit of which is pastoral charity.

The pedagogical and methodological goal of such a contemplative theology is to foster affectively imbued minds that *think in prayer*.[5] To think in prayer means that one's noetic structures are vulnerable to the beauty of revelation, a beauty that is carried to one within the very Person of Christ. So the intellect, the traditional matrix of truth, becomes deeply related to the affect and will, the traditional powers of good and of love. The intellect is formed to receive and then delight in the truth, which impresses itself upon the mind when the mind is fascinated with the holy. The source for such intellectual fascination is *vulnerability to intimacy* with that which is beyond us ... God as truth and beauty, God as longing satisfied. When men live their lives as prayer, as lives of a sacred exchange between their freedom and God's own self-offering in Christ, then they begin to move from the mind they have now to a new mind. They allow the mind of Christ to possess them, and they begin to think in new ways; they allow Him to "think in [them]" as Jean Pierre de Caussade radically phrased it.[6]

Such a source of theology can also have usefulness since "beauty is not opposed to" usefulness. "Beauty applies to and arises within the being that possesses it. It is related to the

truth of things.... The beautiful is a sign of our human finite-
ness. It is part of our glory that we can be receptive to what
is not of ourselves yet is somehow still addressed to us."[7] The
acknowledgement and reception of Divine love suspends the
normal academic way of looking at things and opens before us
a singular way of learning; a learning by beholding, a beholding born of communion. From this communion, this state of
prayer, we then endeavor to express intelligibly the contents
of such beholding, the contents of a seeing that culminates in
communion. This would be the activity of the classroom.

Once removed from this immediate dwelling in the
Word, we then begin to reflect upon what others have said
about such beholding in communion, and so derivative commentary and critique of texts follow. This process crispates,
however, if each theologian does not approach his or her own
study and teaching as acts of vulnerability capable of receiving
God. We are not, in other words, to think that *the nature* of
immediate dwelling in the Word *is separate* from the reflection upon this truth when we study or teach. Without this
personal beholding, this "holding" and "being held" by the
Mystery, we cannot progress to *think in prayer*. Such thinking is not metaphorical or to be understood as "poetic" in a
scientifically dismissive or impatient way. Rather, to think
in prayer means to welcome a deeper beauty, one *that thinking itself* elicits due to the professor abiding in communion
with Christ.[8]

A More Generous Definition of Human Reason

> Certainly, love, as Saint Paul says, "tran-
> scends" knowledge and is thereby capable of
> perceiving more than thought alone (cf. Eph
> 3:19); nonetheless, it continues to be love of
> the God who is *Logos*. Consequently, Chris-
> tian worship is ... worship in harmony with
> the eternal Word and with our reason (cf.
> Rom 12:1).... The intention here is not one
> of retrenchment or negative criticism, but of
> broadening our concept of reason and its ap-
> plication.... Reason and faith come together
> in a new way, if we overcome the self-imposed
> limitation of reason to the empirically falsifi-
> able, and if we once more disclose its vast ho-
> rizons. In this sense, theology rightly belongs
> in the university ... not merely as a historical
> discipline and one of the human sciences, but
> precisely as theology, as inquiry into the ra-
> tionality of faith.[9]

Faith and reason are to heal one another.[10] "The rational principle has revealed itself as love, as that greater reason which accepts into itself even ... irrationality and heals
[it]."[11] In the seminary context, faith and reason are to enter
into a mutually interpenetrating colloquy aiming to end
the seclusion of spirituality within the internal forum and
theology's seclusion within the critical realm. Within their
teaching and study, how do theologians enter this mystery
of a love that heals irrationality? Spiritual direction, with its
necessary gift of confidentiality, cannot be the defining image for spirituality in the seminary; spirituality, communion

with Christ, is not "private." Secular academic methodology, summarized in the words "critical approach," cannot exhaust the work of reason in the seminary. One may ask, "What is the reasonableness of contemplative prayer? What is the reasonableness of affective movements of the heart during the Eucharistic liturgy?" Reason can "behold" and engage these realities, not simply in dispassionate ways but from within a deep communion with them. From such engagement, the participant coaxes out truths, truths that are carried by symbols, affections, gestures, signs.

Where is the light that bears the truth within what theologians study? What aspect of our study carries the "living reality" of our existing in communion with the Trinity?[12] If we think in such ways, ways that facilitate our thinking in prayer, the character of our thoughts will be differentiated from the strictly academic, thus embodying a more generous understanding of reason. As Congar noted, there is always the danger in academic theology that it "risks becoming no longer [about] things essentially religious but more or less rational propositions."[13] To think in prayer is to reverence what Bernard Lonergan called the *eros of the mind*.[14] The theologian desires the truth; he or she wants to taste it and ultimately rest in it. Ultimately, this desire is for Christ, and so the thinker wants to do more than think; he or she wants union with what he or she loves, the living God. There is a distinction, of course, between what one is studying and teaching in theology and the Person of Christ. However, it does not follow that Christ *cannot* communicate His love through specific theological concepts. For the theologian, the mind is desiring more than an idea (the eros of the mind), always more than an idea; he or she desires the reception of Truth as Person to Love.

One interpenetrating reality shared by those in academic formation and those in spiritual formation is the cultivation and nourishment of this eros of the mind. The truth itself is compelling. In spiritual direction, a director spends a lot of time trying to stay out of the way of God, allowing God to bring the truth, in all its personal power and beauty, to the directee. In order for seminarians to begin thinking in prayer, a professor may have to spend at least some of his or her class time "staying out of the way" of God.[15] We want the seminarian to become vulnerable to the truth and beauty of revelation; to think in a way that communicates this truth to others. He is to cultivate a mind that prays, a mind that thinks out of his own communion with Christ. In so doing, he invites others not simply into the nature of things but into their ordering and goal. In the future, receiving a theological degree from a seminary will mean that such a graduate has begun to think in prayer. A successful graduate, under the tutelage of professors and spiritual directors who have been formed in such thinking as well, will be competent to lead others into a fascination with the holy, and not simply into an intellectual examination of the holy. Such a graduate will endeavor to provoke conversion of mind and heart in his parishioners. He will do this by being a man who thinks in prayer, whose own cogitations emanate from his intimate communion with Christ. In a future academic environment where the spiritual is sublated into the discursive, and the discursive opens up deep silences of divine intimacy, we will prepare men to say, "Yes," to Christ's own invitation to take on His mind (1 Cor. 2:16).

One day, hopefully, formators at the doctoral or license level will be eager to form theologians in ways that promote the education of the mystical-pastoral priest. Currently, in their training, future professors undergo a discipline ordered toward the attainment of logical accuracy, skills of appropriating critical methodology, and a creativity that communicates research findings in an innovative way. To be called to teach in a seminary program that sees spiritual formation as its heart (PPF 115), academicians must also learn to suffer the *integration of love and truth*, not in separate cloisters (chapel vs. classroom, internal forum vs. external forum) but in the *very activity* of study, lecture, and testing. And those who administer spiritual formation must suffer the coming of this integration *in the very directing of seminarians* to receive healing and truth in the love of Christ. In this way, in the spiritual forum, the seminarian and director will aid to secure and deepen a love for truth in the contemplative study of theology. As then Cardinal Ratzinger argued, "Rationality belongs to the very essence of Christianity."[16] If rationality belongs to the essence of Christianity, then it belongs to the essence of priestly formation; and it must find its proper expression both academically and spiritually. This "rationality," however, is not to be understood in the way post-enlightenment European universities conceived of it.[17] Closer to our approach would be what Bonaventure noted:

> For faith elevates one to assent (to what is to be believed); (the gifts of) knowledge and

understanding elevate one to understand what has been believed.... It must be said that when it is assented to *on account of reason itself*, then the place of faith is destroyed, because in the soul of a man the violence of reason dominates. But when faith does not assent on account of reason, but on account of love of Him to whom it assents, it desires to have reasons; then human reason does not remove merit, but increases consolation.[18]

Here, in Bonaventure's comments on teaching theology, we find principles that are common to both spiritual direction and teaching; we approach interior intimacy with God by way of faith, but we know our loving faith in God gives birth to the desire to know Him more. Of course, in spiritual direction, the Holy Spirit makes the obscure clear by having the directee attend to both the affective movements of his heart and the accompanying images that may be present. In theology, the theologian labors to reach clarity with the powers of his or her love-imbued mind; he or she then shares the fruit of this labor with the class. There ought not to be, however, a separation between his or her study and teaching and intimacy with the Holy Spirit. Theology is not contemplation and then teaching; it is contemplation even *in* teaching, contemplation even *in* research. In theology, as well as in spiritual direction, we are invited to yield to the Spirit in the very actions of our duties.

If we are to see, to understand, we must lean on the experts in prayer, not only the experts in language and history and pedagogical method. Seminary theologians should seek out spiritual directors and begin a colloquy on prayer for the particular purpose of becoming better theologians.

> A participation in the mind of Jesus, i.e. in His prayer, which is an act of love, of self-giving and self-expropriation to men, is not some kind of pious supplement to the reading the Gospels.... On the contrary, it is the basic pre-condition if real understanding...is to take place.... The person who prays begins to see ... love is the faculty of seeing.... All real progress in theological understanding has its origin in the eye of love and its faculty of beholding.[19]

Here, we desire to build up our faculty of seeing, our power of loving whom we study. And spiritual directors should converse with theologians in order to deepen their desire to learn what knowledge is unleashed in the prolonged contemplation of the Paschal Mystery. Without theology, spiritual directors can be tempted to reduce their activities to techniques; with a theological mind, the spiritual director becomes free to allow the directee to enter prayer and its contents right in his presence. And because of his love of theology, he can give assistance where needed in the exploration of how divine truth attaches itself to affective movements of the heart. The theologian needs to explore how the affective movements of the heart carry divine truth.

If we are to think in prayer and recover a more generous understanding of the function of reason, then a dialogue is to be initiated between spiritual formation and intellectual formation so that professors become experts in suffering divine realities and not simply in learning about them. Christ did not only want to say a word to us, but He also wanted us to know what He was saying in prayer to His Father. When we rest on the heart of Christ, we are also resting upon what Christ is resting upon (Jn 1:18).[20] In a plentiful way, we *want* to be affected by what our love-imbued mind rests upon. Here is what distinguishes a seminary theology from a secular theology: we desire to know—and not simply to understand, to receive the meaning of texts—so that our intimacy with God is deepened. We are to live in the Spirit as we study and teach, in union with the One who searches the deep things of God.

> The Spirit does not spiritualize what is earthly but manifests the limitless self-revelation of God that lies in what is incarnate.... This happens not in the timelessness of a general philosophical or scientific truth *but when its uniquely historical and at the same time unsurpassable timeliness gets through to me*, provided I expose myself to being affected by it.[21]

Theology encounters a living Being and becomes love-filled fascination. It will be the transmission of this fascination and only this that truly enables the future priest to sustain any interest in remaining an intellectual. Without *this spark of fascination* born of a study vulnerable to a living Presence, the rush of pastoral duty will dull his mind and weaken his will to delight in contemplation and meditation, thus reducing his preaching of the Word to relevant moralism.

Fr. Todd Lajiness, dean of Sacred Heart Seminary, has expressed similar ideas:

> It is only through repeated encounters with the Lord that intellectual formation moves from an exercise of the mind to an integration with the heart. It is the deliberate process whereby we actively journey with the Lord and allow him to approach us, to speak to us, and to reveal himself to us through study and prayer. This is what Pope John Paul II meant when he wrote "intellectual formation is to be integrated with a spirituality marked by a personal experience with God. In this way a purely abstract approach to knowledge is overcome."[22] The encounter of the two disciples [on the road to Emmaus, Lk 24] is an example of the way in which intellectual formation can unfold in the mind and the heart of the student, not through the encounter with abstract principles, but rather, through the transformative encounter with Christ himself.[23]

More time is needed for prayer within our study than time needed to actually teach. Teaching becomes plentiful, rich, effective when it flows from communion with Christ. Such communion does not deflate the powers of the intellect but disposes it for creativity and connectivity.[24] I am emphasizing that our communion with Christ is received and sustained right within our study and teaching of theology to underscore that such intimacy is not extraordinary or elitist; we just need to be conscious of its reality so as to receive it. "The Word became flesh and has never taken Himself back into something purely spiritual.... We need not acquire any other 'spiritual senses' for savoring God than those God has given us."[25]

Can we be more intentional about asking seminarians this question? "How has this class deepened your relationship with God?" Can theology be authentic if it aims to foster and develop a relationship with God analogous to the way spiritual directors see their role? We do not create the relationship, but within our efforts to teach the truths about God, we can develop that relationship.[26] And most vitally, this relationship with God will deepen in theology only if we free the students *to listen for His presence within the contents of theology* and invite them to respond (by a more deeply receptive study of theology). The key here is *to stop isolating the coming of God from our thinking about God.*[27] Such resistance to His coming thwarts the development of seminarians from becoming theologians *for life,* producing ones who simply earn academic degrees.

Notes

1   *The Gifts of the Holy Spirit*, trans. Dominic Hughes OP, (New York: Sheed and Ward, 1950), Chapter 4.

2   Jean-Louis Bruguès, Secretary of the Congregation for Catholic Education (Zenit.org and *l'Osservatore Romano,* August. 19, 2009).

3   Reason exists not only within one's relationship with Christ but within a communal context; we know the truths of faith not by simply gazing from afar in a stance of "objectivity," but through participation in the ecclesial and human community. Another avenue to explore in dialogue with spiritual formation is the ecclesial and anthropological: What communal truths define the seminary, inclusive of those that define the Church, and point to a more specific mission of the seminary? Could they be the very identities of the priest himself—spouse, physician, shepherd, father—and the very identities of a man—son, brother, spouse, father? What influence do these identities play in the way that we reason in the seminary, in the way that we think about the theology that we present, the counsel that we dispense, the prayer that we pray, and the charity that we share?

4   Yves Congar, *A History of Theology* (NY: Doubleday, 1968) 104ff. I would place my approach more in line with the Augustinian-Bonaventurian approach that promotes theology's direct reference to God and knowledge and love of Him.

5   See, Gavin D'Costa, *Theology in the Public Square* (Oxford: Blackwell, 2005) 130 for some interesting meditations on prayer as theological method. See also, "Since the object of theology is the Truth which is the living God and His plan for salvation revealed in Jesus Christ, the theologian is called to deepen his own life of faith and continuously unite his scientific research with prayer.(4) In this way, he will become more open to the "supernatural sense of faith" upon which he depends, and it will appear to him as a sure rule for guiding his reflections and helping him assess the correctness of his conclusions." Congregation for the Doctrine of the Faith; *Instruction on the Ecclesial Vocation of the Theologian, 1990, n.8.*

6   Jean Pierre de Caussade, *Treatise on Prayer from the Heart* (St. Louis: Institute of Jesuit Sources, 1998) 145, n. 38.

7   James Schall, SJ, *The Order of Things* (San Francisco: Ignatius, 2007), 206-7.

8   Ibid, 208.

9   Benedict VXI, "Meeting with the Representatives of Science Lecture," University of Regensburg, September 12, 2006.

10   Tracey Rowland, *Ratzinger's Faith* (NY: Oxford, 2008) 119.

11   John M. McDermott, SJ, "Joseph Ratzinger on Faith and Reason," *Angelicum* (86) 2009, 587.

12   Mark McIntosh, *Discernment and Truth* (NY: Herder, 2004) 20.

13   Yves Congar, *The History of Theology* (NY: Doubleday, 1968) 141. Congar noted this about Martin Luther's approach to theology. "Luther's theology is pious, heartfelt theology in which there is no question of dissecting objects by knowledge but simply of clinging to them in a warm, consoling faith." (152) Is this the type of theology I am calling for? Yes and No. I would note that what is true, I want to cling to, and what is "new," I want to dissect. I see little point to dissecting critically what is dogmatically true. Theology achieved such an articulation of truth after arduous thought and prayer, confirmed by the inspired Magisterium of the Church. What would be the service rendered to the salvation of the Church to spend one's days dismantling what is healing and true (e.g., the divinity of Christ, His resurrection, the Real Presence of Christ in the Eucharist, etc?). Certainly we want to understand what is true, and to do so will take a discerning cogent analysis of doctrine. Even good activities like study can get in the way of our search for holiness if they are powered by self-will. See also 155-56 and the discussion on the "science of conclusions."

14   James Connor, SJ, *The Dynamism of Desire* (MO; St. Louis : Institute for Jesuit Sources, 2006), 44.

15   Ibid., 55.

16   Joseph Ratzinger, *The Nature and Mission of Theology* (San Francisco: Ignatius, 1995), 56.

17   The great revolution in these matters took place mainly in the late nineteenth and early twentieth centuries. Germany was the *locus classicus* for the development, but it was imitated and eventually surpassed by American Universities. For the German development and its impact on wider educational matters, look at the work of Fritz Ringer; *The Decline of the German Mandarins* and *The Rise of the Modern Educational System*. The classic work on the development of the American University system is Laurence Veysey, *The Emergence of the American University*. Also: Bruce Kimball, *Orators and Philosophers*; Christopher Jencks and David Riesman, *The Academic Revolution*.

18   St. Bonaventure, *Sentences*, q. 2 conclu. N. 5.

19   Joseph Ratzinger, *Behold the Pierce One* (San Francisco: Ignatius, 1986) 27. "Whoever wishes to be a theologian cannot just count on his intelligence, but must cultivate a profound experience of faith . . . true knowledge is never the fruit of aseptic thoughts, but of contemplative intuition." Benedict XVI, General Audience, September 23, 2009.

20   Hans Urs von Balthasar, *Christian Meditation* (Ignatius: San Francisco, 1989), 17.

21   Ibid., 30.

22   John Paul II, *Pastores Dabo Vobis* (1992), 51.

23   Father Todd Lajiness, "A Passion for Christ: Pedagogical Considerations for Roman Catholic Seminary Intellectual Formation" Forthcoming, *Seminary Journal*.

24   See, Balthasar, *Meditations*, 47.

25   Ibid., 53; "To know much and taste nothing—of what use it that" St Bonaventure, Hexaem. Xxiii, 21.

26   See, William Barry and William Connolly, *The Practice of Spiritual Direction* (NY: Harper, Revised edition 2009), 31-32.

27   Ibid., 35.

The Love of Learning in the Life of the Diocesan Priest

Father Thomas McDermott, OP, STD

"I will rise now and go about the city,
in the street and in the squares;
I will seek him whom my soul loves."

Song of Songs 3:2

I recently attended a retreat for seminarians preached by a brother priest. When he began his first conference, my ears perked up. I was hearing something that was different. This was someone who was not repeating clichés or hammering us with moral exhortations ("You have to...!") but, instead, someone who had obviously prepared by reading, thinking, and praying. Someone who had a fresh perspective on old truths and their application in our day; someone whose message was *life-giving*. In the course of his talk, he mentioned that, several years ago, as a busy diocesan priest, he had decided to remove the television from his bedroom and to use the time that he normally spent in front of it reading spiritual works. The fruits of his decision became more obvious to me in the course of the retreat.

Today's seminarians are much more interested in the spiritual life, contemplative prayer, and traditional practices like the rosary and adoration of the Blessed Sacrament than my generation of twenty-five years ago. In the long history of Christian spirituality, there has sometimes been a degree of suspicion that too much intellectual activity could undermine one's piety; although, on the whole, the "great tradition" has recognized that we cannot love something that we do not know and that if our love for God is meant to increase, then our knowledge must somehow also increase.

Today, we live in a culture that has been impinged by nihilism, the deadly belief that life is ultimately meaningless and, thus, going nowhere. As a result, many have lost confidence in the value of reason and the importance of study. If life is meaningless, then what is the point of studying? Studying assumes the opposite: that life has meaning and coherence. Another contemporary problem is that we can feel buried beneath so much information that we despair of ever arriving at much, if any, understanding in the midst of so many facts. Everyone, including Catholic seminarians, is influenced in one way or another by the dominant culture in which we live.

Perhaps, many newly-ordained priests, when they hear of life-long study, think of the drudgery of learning Hebrew or Greek or some other subject in the seminary and

may say something like, "Most of what I learned in the seminary has had little application to life in a parish." Perhaps
you have heard of priests who have been described as "not
having opened a book since seminary." Yet, secular culture
places great emphasis on constant professional development
so as to remain current and effective. I wonder how many of
the lay faithful have quietly walked away from the Church
because they did not think that their pastor, in his homilies
and pastoral initiatives, had anything fresh or meaningful
to offer or that he was as clueless as they were about how
Christianity makes any difference in day-to-day life. Perhaps
in eternity, God will show us priests the awful answer to
that question.

In the rite of ordination, priests are obliged to be
"mature in learning." The desire for ongoing learning in the
life of the priest is actually a response to the grace of ordination, as well as to God's call for daily conversion. John Paul
II challenged seminary teachers and formators to prepare
seminarians for ongoing formation after ordination:

> Long term preparation for ongoing forma-
> tion should take place in the major seminary,
> where encouragement needs to be given to
> future priests to look forward to it, seeing
> its necessity, its advantages and the spirit in
> which it should be undertaken, and appro-
> priate conditions for its realization need to
> be ensured.[1]

How can we, as seminary educators, formators, and spiritual
directors, cultivate a life-long desire of learning in the lives of
future diocesan priests?

Such a desire cannot happen without a living, authentic love of God and a desire for Him. Desire, a venerable theme in the history of Catholic spirituality, means a deep longing to be united with God in a perfect communion of intellect and will. Desire also implies an urgent and loving willingness to work for the salvation of others, with the help of God's grace, since to love God means to love what He loves.[2] Study without desire is lifeless and leads nowhere, but study fueled by desire leads to pleasure and joy. Love and desire, however, do not arise from a vacuum but rather, from knowledge, especially *knowledge of ourselves* and *knowledge of God.*

Catherine of Siena, the great Doctor of the Church, could neither read nor write but she had a great love of learning and study. She would "pick the brain" of any learned person she met, often staying up late at night discussing theological topics with priests and scholars. She had a "sacred curiosity," the curiosity a lover has of one's beloved, but hers was about all things divine. Catherine understood well that knowledge always changes us: whatever we know acts upon us in some way. The mind is always being formed, or transformed, by knowledge. But what kind of knowledge do we give it? Think of the hours the average American spends watching television every week. Whether we are watching sports or a movie, the subject matter has a formative effect on our minds—even if it only numbs them. Catherine also knew that defective knowledge leads invariably to defective love of self, others, and God.

Let us turn first to knowledge of ourselves as human beings. The first thing to note, according to the saints and mystics, is our poverty. We have nothing of our own; everything we have is God's gift, and apart from Him, we would simply cease to exist. "What do you have," asks St. Paul, "that you did not receive?" (1 Cor 4:7). Moreover, sin has made us all prodigal sons existing in a state of exile far from the Father's house, starving for purpose and meaning in an alien place, blind to the truth. Salvatorian Father Bernard Green says that "sin derives from our mysterious ability for sustaining a radical self-deception in which we avoid recognition of who we really are and what it is we want, leading to mistreatment of ourselves and one another."[3] And it was Thomas Merton who said that "the soul that is only dimly enlightened by God has very little conception of its own [spiritual] indigence."[4] But when we really know the truth about ourselves, there will well up in us a tremendous sense of *need*. Knowing our poverty and need is the first step toward the experience of a blessed freedom which Jesus was referring to when He said, "The truth shall make you free," and, "Blessed are the poor in spirit (Jn 8:32 and Mt 5:3). Knowing the truth about ourselves ought to impel us to seek the truth.

If we were to stop at only knowledge of ourselves, we might fall into despair. St. Catherine says that knowledge of our poverty must *always* be held together with knowledge of God. What do we need to know about God? We need to know that He made us unlike any other creature, in His own image and likeness, so that He could share with us His divine life. Although we are quite literally "nothing" apart from our Creator, we are, by His grace (quite literally) precious, important, and loved.

It is good to remind ourselves of who we are apart from God, but we must always quickly move ahead and see ourselves through the eyes of Jesus Christ, "the human face of God." A caution: This does not mean that we "know" God in and of Himself, in a comprehensive way, in the very mystery of the Godhead which St. Catherine often refers to as an "abyss." In the days before the Second Vatican Council, altar frontals sometimes were inscribed with the Latin words *Deus absconditus,* "God hidden," unknowable by the human mind. St. Thomas Aquinas famously said that we cannot know what God is but only what He is not. "Neither a Catholic nor a pagan," St. Thomas says, "knows the nature of God as he is in himself."[5] To say that there is much about God we do not know is an extreme understatement! Long ago, in 1215, the fourth Lateran Council stated that however great the similarity that may be established between Creator and creature, the dissimilarity between them is always greater.

Should we despair of knowing God? No, if by "knowing" we do not mean a comprehensive knowledge of him. Our faith, then, is faith in a "veiled God"—we can see His outlines; we can know what is necessary for our voluntary return to Him, but we can never totally see Him as He is. Perhaps, at times, we have all tried to trivialize or "domesticate" God by removing this sense of His unknowability. It would be wrong, as Father Green says, to take advantage of God's humility and thereby "draw the curtains on His presence, so that we might never know a greater being than ourselves. In doing so, we progressively lose our own being."[6] God as an infinite "abyss" who knows us and loves us to the point of death should be a stimulus for us to come closer to the mystery, particularly through study and prayer. Not to do so, we run the risk of fossilizing.

From knowledge of the truth about ourselves and about God naturally spring love for Him and desire to know more and love more. This desire should bring us to a renewed interest in the Word of God or Holy Scripture. The priest who values life-long study and learning is characterized by attentiveness to the Word of God. John Paul II reminds us that the priest "is not the master of the Word, but its servant."[7] In fact, the Word of God can *never* be mastered. Dominican Father Timothy Radcliffe talks of the "thrilling discovery that we do not know what this text means."[8] Yet how many of us preachers prefer to pass over difficult or unclear texts which would require some study on our part and then fall back into preaching on clearer parts of a text on which we have preached a hundred times, bringing out once again the proverbial "old chestnut"?

Besides Scripture, seminarians and priests often read history of one type or another, for example, the life of a particular saint or other figure. This is a good practice because history, as the historian Owen Chadwick points out, "does more than any other discipline to free the mind from the tyranny of present opinion."[9] Reading secular books is not to be discouraged so long as we are determined to find truth, which always has its source in the Holy Spirit, wherever it may be found. Aquinas encourages us to be like St. Paul who quoted many non-Jewish sources by rejecting the bad parts of secular literature and keeping the good. He supports his argument in a rather quaint medieval fashion: he cites Deuteronomy 21 which states that if a man sees a young woman among the captives, he should trim her nails and hair and take her home. In other words, remove all that is superfluous and keep what is true![10]

The habit of life-long learning is an indication that the theological virtue of hope is actuated in us. Study, like prayer, is an act of hope. Father Sertillanges, in his famous work *The Intellectual Life*, says that study is a form of "active prayer."[11] Those of us who are teachers or formators in seminaries ought to impress on our students that *the habit of life-long learning is an important aid to holiness.* Study or "sacred curiosity" is a path to holiness. "If a man perfectly submits his learning and his other powers to God," says St. Thomas, "his devotion, as a direct result, will be deepened."[12] The vital connection between knowledge and holiness needs to be stressed over and over again in our seminaries, starting at the outset of priestly formation.

There can be no love of God without knowledge, and neither knowledge nor love can remain static—if they are not increasing, they are decreasing. There is no standing still in the spiritual life, as St. Catherine herself says: "The soul cannot but move: If she does not go forward, she turns back."[13] Frantic pastoral activity without an increase in knowledge and love will end, unfortunately, where it started, as Father Edward Leen wrote in his classic work *The Holy Spirit* in 1939:

> If then men's striving [has] not as [its] consequence a growth in knowledge and love of God, [it is] fruitless and vain. Their gropings after "life" are thwarted. They may move from point to point on the earth's surface with ever

greater speed, but their movement brings them to no position of rest or satiety.... Such movement brings men nowhere. The activity that brings men to the experience of having got somewhere, of having moved to some purpose, of having aimed at a goal which marks a progress in life, is the movement of the soul toward God in *knowledge and love*.[14]

Knowledge and love are the arms by which we are united with God, with the help of His grace.

Father Leen goes on to say that the Holy Spirit imparts to us the "heavenly mind," initiating us "into the knowledge of divine things." The Spirit comes to us "laden with all the secrets of God," eager to communicate to the soul the supernatural gifts of understanding (the gift of insightful faith) and knowledge (the gift of mature faith).[15] Knowledge of God opens the way for *communion with* Him. In fact, knowledge of God that does not lead to this communion is pointless. Communion with God requires another gift of the Holy Spirit: wisdom. Wisdom allows us to know God not so much in a cognitive way but in an affective or experiential way, with a "love-knowledge," the knowledge lovers have of one another. When the saints and mystics speak of "tasting" God's presence, it is because they have generously opened themselves to receiving the gift of wisdom, which leads to deification and union with God. The Church recognizes wisdom as the highest gift of the Holy Spirit.

Father Jacques Philippe, in his modern spiritual classic *Interior Freedom*, speaks of the "three outpourings of the Spirit": to illumine and reveal, to strip and impoverish, and to confirm and fortify.[16] Self-knowledge reflects the work of the Holy Spirit in stripping us of our self-deceptions and exposing our poverty. Knowledge of God and of truth is a result of the Spirit's illumining and revealing the truth to us. The Spirit of Truth does not reveal new truths but sheds new light on eternal truths. The Holy Spirit is not only the Spirit of Truth, which, as such, pertains to the intellect, but also the Spirit of Love, which elevates the will or the heart. The Spirit draws us, in Christ, with our outstretched arms of knowledge and love, into the eternal embrace of the Father where we will be "filled with the utter fullness of God" (Eph 3:19).

The habit of life-long learning leads to the continual transformation of the heart. Learning and study in the life of the priest are not meant to be mind-games or a matter of merely collecting information or remembering facts. The Spirit of Truth elevates our human knowledge, giving us "a new heart" and "a new spirit." Father Green puts it this way:

> Growth in holiness, therefore, does depend upon a deepening of knowledge, but it is not speculative knowledge ... but that knowledge of another which comes through relationships. Such "saving knowledge" is indeed the goal of the spiritual life but only because this knowledge is intrinsically linked to love which reaches out to the neighbor in need whoever he or she might be.[17]

St. Teresa of Avila regarded learning as an *essential* requirement of any priest who would do spiritual direction. In fact, she says forthrightly that she always preferred "learned priests" to "pious ones": "Half-learned confessors have done

my soul great harm when I have been unable to find a confessor with as much learning as I like.... A truly learned man
has never misguided me."[18] And: "Spiritual but unlearned
directors were cramped by their own experience, they knew
only one way to be Christian.... But learned directors ... were
more free to recognize as legitimate ways of being Christian
which were not part of the prevailing ethos."[19]

The commitment to study and learning is a renewal
and reaffirmation of the priest's "Yes, at ordination that has
a direct bearing on the quality of his service to the People
of God. From the moment of the priest's ordination, John
Paul II says, "begins that response which, as a fundamental
choice, must be expressed anew and reaffirmed through the
years of his priesthood in countless other responses, all of
them rooted in and enlivened by that 'yes' of Holy Orders."[20]
He goes on to say that the priest has an obligation to the
People of God to engage in ongoing, permanent formation:

> Permanent formation is a requirement of the
> priest's own faithfulness to his ministry, to
> his very being. It is love for Jesus Christ and
> fidelity to oneself. But it is also an act of love
> for the People of God, at whose service the
> priest is placed. Indeed, an act of true and
> proper justice: The priest owes it to God's
> people, whose fundamental "right" to receive
> the word of God, the sacraments and the ser-
> vice of charity, the original and irreplaceable
> content of the priest's own pastoral ministry,
> he is called to acknowledge and foster. Ongo-
> ing formation is necessary to ensure that the
> priest can properly respond to this right of
> the People of God.[21]

Almost every diocese or region organizes study days or workshops for its priests. Some priests rarely, if ever, attend, while others seldom miss such opportunities for personal growth.

What factors mitigate against the habit of life-long learning, and what can we, as seminary educators, formators and spiritual directors, do to overcome them? I would like to focus on five factors in the hope that once we expose and identify them in our teaching and formation work, they will lose some of their force in the lives of seminarians.

First, we must recognize that spiritual growth, of which learning is a component, can be extremely difficult. No doubt, the influence of various contemporary secular and quasi-religious spiritualities and self-help programs has seduced many into thinking that spiritual growth is easy, and even fun. But, as Father Green notes,

> The heart rarely wants to be disturbed. Much of our psychological patterning is to avoid disturbing our inner selves. We involve ourselves much more easily in self-justification and rationalization than in changing.... [I]n so many ways, we fear the changes which growth demands and avoid recognizing our need for it and the occasions which might demand it of us.[22]

To grow spiritually involves a dying to self, which is, by nature, abhorrent to us. Ultimately, the underlying reason for difficulty in growing spiritually is the resistance of our created wills to grace which, as Father Leen says, "may proceed from want of spiritual enlightenment" so that failure to develop spiritually may more often than not "be attributed not to bad will but to an imperfect understanding" or, in other words, to a lack of knowledge.[23]

The acquisition of the habit of life-long learning requires an act of the will, just like fasting and other forms of mortification. In fact, learning as a means to holiness is a type of asceticism. Many young people today are attracted to a Christianity which makes demands and are willing to participate in fasts and vigils. Teachers, formators, and spiritual directors should remind seminarians that an important but often overlooked ascetical practice is study. "What are you reading now?" is a question which should often be asked in seminaries.

The second factor that stands in the way of life-long learning is that modern men and women are accustomed to constant noise of one form or another and are uncomfortable with silence and solitude. The first few hours of a silent retreat can be almost terrifying for some people. It was recently reported that many young Americans today fear being alone more than anything else. But solitude and silence are necessary elements of the spiritual life, not only for the sake of prayer but also for study, which often precedes prayer. Discomfort with solitude exposes our inability to listen well—to God and to others. The ability to truly discuss something with others and to pay attention to what others are saying is increasingly difficult for us today. Awareness of these facts, however, can be the first step to change. Seminary days of recollection and retreats are ideal opportunities for extended periods of silence. Other days and times could also be set aside as silent periods. One place that study as a means to holiness can take place is during the daily holy hour.

Also, instructors could begin simply by inserting into the class period a few minutes of silence[24] before or after considering a truth of the faith, reminiscent of God's command to Moses at the burning bush: "Come no nearer! Remove the sandals from your feet, for the place where you stand is holy ground" (Ex 3:5).

Third, the temptation in pastoral ministry to a shallow activism, sometimes an attempt to control anxiety, also mitigates against a spirituality of study. John Paul II warns priests against the "temptation to reduce ministry to an activism which becomes an end in itself ... or to a business-like function which [they carry] out for the Church."[25] An overworked pastor who was preoccupied with parish administration was once described by his associate as being "good *to* the people, but not necessarily *for* the people." Pastoral activity, which is not grounded in a vital relationship with the Lord, produces fruits which do not "endure for eternal life" (Jn 6:27). To be "good for the people" and not merely pleasant to them requires a real spiritual life which has the thirst for learning as one of its sources. Priests must consider contemplation not as an obstacle to getting things done but as a necessary part of priestly ministry. For many priests, this will mean fixing a specific time every day for study or the holy hour and rarely allowing exceptions.

Fourth, failure to acquire the habit of learning may reflect an excessive trust in himself and in his own pastoral experience which, as John Paul says, can lead a priest "to presume he can manage on his own, as if his own personal experience, which has seemed trustworthy to that point, needs no contact with anything or anyone else."[26] The theological virtue of hope enables us to trust in the power and grace of God instead of ourselves to save us. Hope is perfected by the gift of "fear of the Lord" or wonder and awe before the majesty and splendor of God who is totally "other." Hope opposes the vice of presumption in which "man presumes upon his own capacities."[27] The grip that excessive self-trust has on us can be weakened through a habit of regular confession, attending fraternal gatherings of priests or annual retreats or diocesan convocations and study days, choosing a spiritual director who is not afraid to challenge us, and creating ways for the laity to give us honest and constructive feedback.

Fifth, resistance to a life-long habit of learning may reflect, as a document from one of the recent general chapters of the Dominican Order states, "the false hope of faith without ambiguity."[28] Benedict XVI has spoken at some length of the "mystery of God" and the "silence of God": "One can still ask why God did not make a world in which his presence is more evident—why Christ did not leave the world with another sign of his presence so radiant that no one could resist it. This is the mystery of God and man, which we find so inscrutable."[29] In the face of such uncertainty, the seminarian may be tempted to seek refuge in a fundamentalism that "takes the form of an unthinking repetition of received words, a refusal to take part in the never ending search for understanding, an intolerance of all for whom tradition is not just a revelation but also an invitation to draw nearer to the mystery."[30] As said earlier, we can never have a comprehensive knowledge of God; we can never know everything that there is to know about Him. We do a disservice to God and to ourselves when we strip divinity of all mystery. Humility and a sense of awe before the mystery should result naturally from our study.

Theology taught in seminaries tends to be *kataphatic* theology—positive theology, that is, "What God is." But the tradition of negative theology, *apophatic* theology, which pertains to the ineffability of God, should be made known in our classrooms. C.S. Lewis, in *Miracles,* advocates that students of theology should first be exposed to apophatic theology in order to cleanse their minds of all misconceptions about God. This could be done very simply by ending class with an excerpt from a spiritual classic such as *The Cloud of the Unknowing* or *Dark Night of the Soul* or one of several passages from Scripture: Ex 3:1-5 (Moses and the burning bush); 1 Kings 19:11-13 (Elijah and the "tiny whispering sound"); 2 Cor 12:2-4 (St. Paul is caught up to the third heaven).

Given the shortage of priests, many in pastoral ministry today feel exhausted and under great stress and complain of too little time to accomplish all that needs to be done. Is it realistic to ask or expect busy diocesan priests to set aside some time for study and learning every week, to use the time that they would normally spend watching television to read or to avail themselves more of continuing educational opportunities, such as study days offered in many dioceses, to consider attending a workshop or study retreat for a few days in the summer, or to simply to read a book? As one who worked for years in parish ministry, let me suggest that a lack of ongoing learning and study may itself be a cause of pastoral fatigue and burnout. Learning can be a remedy for burn-out. Study, just like good music, tends to refresh us; watching television, on the other hand, often enervates us. Study also has the power to address loneliness and pain.

I once lived with two elderly priests. One was never seen reading, not even the daily newspaper. He took no interest in current events and would sit before the television every night for two to three hours watching dramas, comedies, and old movies. All of his interests, recollections, stories, were in the past. In the same priory lived another elderly priest who had a life-long love for learning and who was always reading a book, newspaper, or something on the Internet. If he watched television, it was usually the news or documentaries. Few friars were more current than he was. He was a delight to live with, and young people were attracted to him. Being a life-long lover of learning reflected his desire, even at his advanced age, to learn and grow, which resulted in a youthfulness of spirit, not unlike that of John Paul II who himself said, "Only those who keep ever alive their desire to learn and grow can be said to enjoy this 'youthfulness.'"[31] This youthfulness is the opposite of spiritual sterility and contributes to the fecundity of the priest's spiritual paternity.

As seminary teachers and formators, let us strive to foster a spirituality of learning that does not end at ordination, a spirituality which finds expression in the ancient words of Isaiah the prophet: "*Come, let us climb the LORD's mountain, to the house of the God of Jacob, That he may instruct us in his ways, and we may walk in his paths*" (Isaiah 2:3).

Notes

1   John Paul II, *Pastores Dabo Vobis* (1992), 71.

2   The eternal Father revealed to St. Catherine of Siena that to love Him also means to love what He loves: "The soul, as soon as she comes to know Me, reaches out to love her neighbors." Catherine of Siena, *The Dialogue*. Translated by Suzanne Noffke, OP. *Classics of Western Spirituality* (New York: Paulist Press, 1980), chapter 89, 164-165.

3   Bernard D. Green, SDS. *Death, Sin, and the Gospel.* Catholic Faith and Life Series 3. 2nd ed. (Tempe, AZ: The Institute for the Study of Catholic Faith and Life, 2006), 29.

4   *Spiritual Direction & Meditation* (Collegeville, MN: The order of St. Benedict, 1960), 81.

5   See *Summa theologiae* I-II, q. 3, Pro. and I, q. 13, a. 10, ad. 5.

6   Bernard D. Green, SDS, *The Humility of God. Reflections on the Importance of the Trinity in Christian Experience.* (Tempe, AZ: Institute for the Study of Catholic Faith and Life), 13.

7   John Paul II, *Pastores Dabo Vobis*, 26.

8   Timothy Radcliffe, OP, "The Wellspring of Hope. Study and the Annunciation of the Good News" in *Sing a New Song. The Christian Vocation* (Springfield, IL: Templegate, 1999), 57. I gratefully acknowledge my debt to Fr. Radcliffe for several of his ideas in this essay.

9   Owen Chadwick, *Origins* 1985, 85, quoted in Timothy Radcliffe, OP, "The Wellspring of Hope. Study and the Annunciation of the Good News" in *Sing a New Song. The Christian Vocation* (Springfield, IL: Templegate, 1999), 78.

10   St. Thomas Aquinas, *Sup. Titus 1:15, n. 32,* quoted in Nicholas M. Healy, *Thomas Aquinas. Theologian of the Christian life* (Hants, England: Ashgate, 2003), 41.

11   A.D. Sertillanges, OP., *The Intellectual Life* (Cork, 1965), 71, quoted in Paul Murray, OP, *The New Wine of Dominican Spirituality. A Drink Called Happiness.* (London and New York: Burns & Oates, 2006), 113.

12   St. Thomas Aquinas, *Summa theologiae* II-II, q. 82, a. 3, ad. 3, quoted in Murray, *The New Wine of Dominican Spirituality*, 104. I also wish to express my debt of gratitude to Fr. Murray.

13   *Dialogue*, chapter 4.

14   Edward Leen, C.S.Sp. *The Holy Spirit and His Work in Souls.* Originally published in 1939 by Sheed and Ward. New edition. (New York: Scepter, 1998), 69.

15   Leen, 99 and 128. It is unfortunate that the gifts of the Holy Spirit are so seldom studied in much depth in our seminaries.

16   Jacques Philippe, *Interior Freedom* (New York: Scepter, 2007), 98.

17   Bernard D. Green, SDS. *Christian Spirituality and Human Development. A philosophical and psychological inquiry.* Unpublished manuscript. 122.

18   St. Teresa of Avila, *The Book of Her Life*, Chapter 5, part 3, in *The Collected Works of St. Teresa of Avila.* Vol. 1. Translated by K. Kavanaugh and O. Rodriguez (Washington, DC: ICS Publications, 1987), 71.

19   Quoted in Murray, *The New Wine of Dominican Spirituality*, 114. No citation given.

20   John Paul II, *Pastores Dabo Vobis*, 70.

21   Ibid.

22   Bernard D. Green, SDS. *Death, Sin, and the Gospel.* Catholic Faith and Life Series 4. 2nd ed. (Tempe, AZ: The Institute for the Study of Catholic Faith and Life, 2006), 3, 11.

23   Edward Leen, C.S.Sp. *Progress Through Mental Prayer* (New York: Sheed and Ward, 1935). http://www.ewtn.com/library/SPIRIT/MENTAL.TXT.

24   James Keating, *Resting on the Heart of Christ: The Vocation and Spirituality of the Seminary Theologian* (Omaha: IPF Publications, 2009) 136ff.

25   John Paul II, *Pastores Dabo Vobis*, 72.

26   Ibid., 77.

27   United States Catholic Conference, *Catechism of The Catholic Church* 2092, (Washington D.C.: USCC Publishing, 1997, 2nd Edition).

28   General Chapter of Oakland (CA), no. 109, quoted in Radcliffe, *Sing a New Song*, 61.

29   Joseph Ratzinger [Pope Benedict XVI], *Jesus of Nazareth. From the Baptism in the Jordan to the Transfiguration.* (New York: Doubleday, 2007), 34.

30   Ibid.

31   John Paul II, *Pastores Dabo Vobis*, 79. Cardinal Newman said, "To live is to change, and to be perfect is to change often."

Section 2

Sources of Wisdom

Scripture and Prayer
A Fuller Methodology

Father Thomas J. Lane, STD

The *Program of Priestly Formation*[1] outlines the norms for the intellectual formation of candidates for the priesthood and lists the core Scripture courses for priestly formation in seminary (199). It then specifies how Scripture ought to be properly interpreted—that is, it specifies the methodology seminarians are to learn to exegete the Scriptures:

> The proper understanding of Sacred Scripture requires the use of the historical-critical method, though this method is not totally sufficient. Other methods that are synchronic in approach are helpful in bringing forth the riches contained in the biblical texts.[2]

The *Program of Priestly Formation* concludes its instructions for the teaching of Scripture in seminary by reminding us that it is directed to a pastoral end, "the preparation of seminarians for the tasks of preaching homilies and applying Scripture to the lives of the Christian faithful."[3]

Literary Critical Methods and Teaching Scripture in Seminary

The Historical-Critical Method

The history of the use of the historical-critical method by the Catholic Church for exegesis illustrates why the *Program of Priestly Formation* saw fit to specifically mention it as required at this moment in time. The historical-critical method may be summarized as follows:

> From textual criticism, one progresses to literary criticism, with its work of dissection in the quest for sources; then, one moves to a critical study of forms and, finally, to an analysis of the editorial process, which aims to be particularly attentive to the text as it has been put together. All this has made it possible to understand far more accurately the intention of the authors and editors of the Bible as well as the message which they addressed to their first readers.[4]

This summary also points out the goal of the historical-critical method: more accurate understanding of the mind and intention of the authors and editors of the Bible and thus, their message.

When this method of exegesis first developed following the Renaissance, Catholic involvement was sparse due to this method's origins in the philosophy of the Enlightenment.[5] However, Pope Leo XIII's encyclical *Providentissimus Deus* in 1893 inaugurated the use of scientific methods of critical scholarship in biblical studies. Yet this encyclical could still only be described as an initial opening of the Church to the method. The full acceptance of critical methods in Catholic biblical exegesis occurred in the encyclical *Divino Afflante Spiritu* (1943), published to mark the fiftieth anniversary of *Providentissimus Deus*. Thereafter, we can see the method being advocated in two important documents: *Sancta Mater Ecclesia*, perhaps more often known in English as *The Historicity of the Gospels*, published by the Pontifical Biblical Commission in 1964, and *Dei Verbum* of Vatican II in 1965. Sections 12 and 19 of *Dei Verbum* allude to most of the techniques of the historical-critical method, and *Sancta Mater Ecclesia* (4) invites Catholic exegetes to "make appropriate use of the new exegetical techniques, particularly those advocated by the historical method taken as a whole." Yet it also advised utilizing form criticism with caution since "the method is often interlaced with inadmissible philosophical and theological principles, which frequently vitiate either the method itself or its judgments on literary questions."[6]

The 1980s saw intense debate about the validity of the historical-critical method; and so, the Pontifical Biblical Commission published *The Interpretation of the Bible in the Church* in 1993 to clarify the Church's position with regard to the method and to mark the centenary of *Providentissimus Deus.*[7] *The Interpretation of the Bible in the Church* drew attention to the positive results of the historical-critical method, the limitations of the method, and the necessity of using this method for exegesis, calling it an "indispensable method."[8]

Having surveyed the history of the use of the historical-critical method in the Catholic Church, we see better why the current (fifth) edition of the *Program of Priestly Formation* specifically instructs that the historical-critical method is necessary for proper understanding of Scripture while the previous (fourth) edition of the *Program of Priestly Formation* made no such mention. Seminarians in some houses of formation and seminaries became unreceptive to the historical-critical method due to the excesses of some professors that were seen to detract from the sacredness of Scripture and reduce it to mere human words. Indeed, exaggerated use of the historical-critical method has sometimes in the past brought the method into disrepute. For example, some radical Scripture scholars before the 1960's proposed that Pilate never existed because there was no extra-biblical evidence for his existence, but the discovery of a block of limestone in the Roman theater at Caesarea Maritima in 1961 bearing his name laid to rest any theories of his non-existence. Likewise, there has been an overly cautious approach by some scholars to the historicity of the Pentateuch; but a text discovered at Deir 'Alla in 1967 mentions Balaam, who features in the Book of Numbers. These two examples should give pause to anyone who might suggest that a person mentioned in the Bible did not exist. It took until the 1960s to discover these two significant pieces of extra-biblical evidence, and we might ask how many more biblically significant artifacts are waiting to be discovered. Indeed, such pieces of evidence continue to be found; in 1990, the ossuaries of the family of the high priest Caiaphas were discovered; therefore, any temptation by a seminary professor to use a lack of extra-biblical evidence to discount the biblical narrative is at the very least unwise. At worse, succumbing to such a temptation may show a lack of reverence for the sacred text.

Purification of Method: Interpreting with the Mind of Christ

The previously noted examples of the historical-critical method's imperfections show a need for purification of the method. Pope Benedict XVI, in his address at the University of Regensburg in 2006, called for "broadening our concept of reason and its application"[9] and stated that the dangers facing humanity now can be overcome "only if reason and faith come together in a new way." The 1989 *Instruction on the Study of the Fathers of the Church in the Formation of Priests* (37.1) drew attention to this union of reason and faith in the Church Fathers:

> As theologians they did not rely exclusively on the resources of reason, but also on those (resources) more properly religious, offered by consciousness of an affective and existential character, anchored in intimate union with Christ, nourished by prayer and sustained by grace and the gifts of the Holy Spirit. In their

attitudes as theologians and pastors a profound sense of mystery and experience of the
divine was manifested to the highest degree,
which protected them against ever present
temptations of either an overly driven rationalism or dull and resigned fideism.[10]

The *Instruction on the Study of the Fathers of the
Church in the Formation of Priests* admits that from our
point of view, the exegetical method of the Church Fathers
has some undeniable limits.[11] But the document finds the
Church Fathers to be models of exegetical method for us in
their having a kind of subtle intuition into heavenly things
and a marvelous keenness of intellect, which enabled them
to penetrate more into the inner meaning of the divine
word.[12] Two of the Fathers are put before us as examples of
this interpenetration of reason and faith:[13] St. Gregory, who
in the first of his five theological orations dedicated to the
theological method treats the necessity of moderation, humility, interior purification, and prayer; and St. Augustine,
who, when reflecting on the role of faith in the life of the
Church and theologians, writes that theologians are piously
endowed and truly spiritual. In this sense, *The Program of
Priestly Formation* section 163 states that "because theology
is rooted in the Church's faith and serves the faith of the
Church, it must be studied in complete and faithful communion with the Magisterium."

We could sum up what we are stating by recalling the
principle of St. Thomas Aquinas that grace builds on nature.
In the thirteenth century, reason was preparing to discon-
nect itself from faith. There was the threat of a partition of

the scholarly life into knowledge and faith. "From the point of view of the thirteenth-century 'orthodoxy' ... the attitude of St. Thomas was aggressively unusual and disturbing. For he accepted the opposing positions, both of them, in all their radicality."[14] It is good to be careful of the presuppositions of the historical-critical method because it was informed by rationalistic philosophy, but the historical-critical method can be utilized with the mind of Christ. If it is not utilized with the mind of Christ, what do we derive from our Scripture study? The historical-critical method uses the natural resources of the intellect; but when we include grace, reading Scripture with Christ, then our understanding of Scripture is greatly enriched because we read Scripture bearing in mind what *Dei Verbum* states, that the Scriptures have God as their author and that "the books of Scripture, firmly, faithfully and without error, teach that *truth* which God, *for the sake of our salvation*, wished to see confided to the sacred Scriptures."[15]

Every professor of Scripture encounters seminarians in the classroom who, due to their background or having heard of the immoderation of some professors in the past, are highly suspicious of the historical-critical method without ever having experienced in the classroom how it can aid our understanding of Scripture and who almost consider a professor practicing this method of exegesis as heretical. Very often, seminarians with a mental block to the historical-critical method are thinking only of questions about the historicity of the text; whereas, the historical-critical method involves making use of many techniques useful for bringing out much more of the meaning in the text that the author intended (for example, redaction criticism is especially useful in study of the Synoptic Gospels to demonstrate the unique theology and message of each of the evangelists). The task for the seminary professor in such a situation is to gently lead seminarians, using ecclesial documents, such as those referenced above, and to broaden the rationality of the method—adding grace to nature—so that seminarians can appreciate the benefits of the historical-critical method and overcome their fears and suspicions concerning this approach to the Scriptures. When applying the historical-critical method, it is the integration of reason and faith that saves the seminary professor from choosing an erroneous interpretation because Christ leads us to a fuller embrace of Truth. In this sense, we see that intimacy with Christ is a place of knowing and that faith is a discerning knowledge. It is also the integration of reason and faith when exegeting Scripture that will be useful to the seminarian in his future priestly ministry.

Other Critical Methods

The *Program of Priestly Formation* states, "Other methods that are synchronic in approach are helpful in bringing forth the riches contained in the biblical texts."[16] *The Interpretation of the Bible in the Church* covers a number of synchronic methods of biblical interpretation which examine the Scriptures in their final form in which we now have them rather than in their successive stages of coming into being, as in the case of the diachronic historical-critical method—we might mention, in particular, narrative criticism, rhetorical criticism, and canonical criticism. Narrative criticism or analysis focuses on the narrative as a whole and how the passage in question fits into the entire narrative and how the various strands of the plot all gel together, seeing the links between one passage and the entire biblical book. Thus, passages in the Gospel of Luke take on a new nuance when read in the light of Acts, also authored by Luke. Events in the life of Jesus in the Gospel of Luke can be seen to be remotely preparing for the mission to the Gentiles in Acts. Narrative criticism thus adds another layer of meaning to a text in addition to meaning ascertained by the diachronic historical-critical method. Unlike with the historical-critical method, there is no difficulty in demonstrating to students the necessity of narrative criticism. They are eager for additional narrative criticism. Rhetorical criticism or analysis examines the ability of the biblical text to persuade its reader or listener, and is often applied to passages in the Pauline letters. While narrative criticism analyzes a passage in the context of its entire biblical book, canonical criticism analyzes a passage in the context of the entire Bible, seeking additional meaning that the text did not possess when read in isolation. For example, a number of times in his letters, Paul states that we are saved by faith, as in Rom 3:28, "a person is justified by faith apart from works of the law." But some were perverting Paul's teaching that we are saved by faith and were making it an excuse for not demanding ethical behavior; so James, writing later, corrects this error in Jas 2:14-26, by stating that our faith is expressed in our Christian charity.

As we bring to a close this brief survey of critical methods, we suggest that the *Program of Priestly Formation* makes the following stipulation concerning the teaching of a methodology for exegeting Scripture in seminaries for a good reason—namely, the correct interpretation of Scripture, which is its interpretation according to the mind and intention of the author. The proper understanding of Sacred Scripture requires the use of the historical-critical method, though this method is not totally sufficient. Other methods that are synchronic in approach are helpful in bringing forth the riches contained in the biblical texts.[17]

Scripture and Prayer

We have looked at section 200 of the *Program of Priestly Formation* and its implications for teaching Scripture in seminaries, especially in utilizing literary critical methods to interpret Scripture. Another methodology that needs to be employed in exegesis for a fuller interpretation, and that methodology is prayer. Earlier in the document, the *Program of Priestly Formation* emphasizes spiritual formation as the unifying pillar of formation while the other three pillars of formation are indispensable:

> Since spiritual formation is the core that unifies the life of a priest, it stands at the heart of seminary life and is the center around which all other aspects are integrated. Human, intellectual, and pastoral formation are indispensable in developing the seminarian's relationship and communion with God and his ability to communicate God's truth and love

to others in the likeness of Jesus Christ, the Good Shepherd and eternal High Priest.[18]

It is clear in this paragraph of the *Program of Priestly Formation* that the spiritual and intellectual formation of a seminarian is to be integrated and not autonomous. Spiritual formation "is the core" and intellectual formation is "integrated" into the spiritual formation. The *Program of Priestly Formation* reiterates this point later in the document: "The seminary study of theology, because it begins in faith and ends in faith, must also flow from prayer and lead to prayer."[19] We note that it states that prayer is the source and conclusion of our studies; therefore, we now turn to the integration of intellectual formation, in particular Scripture study, into the spiritual formation of a seminarian.

Integration of Scripture, Study, and Prayer

The *Program of Priestly Formation* is certainly not the first document to draw attention to the necessity of uniting Scripture study with prayer. *Dei Verbum* section 25 encourages priests and all involved in the ministry of the word to diligent and careful study of the Scriptures, "so that none of them will become 'an empty preacher of the Word of God outwardly, who is not a listener to it inwardly.'" We see in this quote an invitation to integrate study and prayer; the ministers of the Word are not only to *study* Scripture but also to *listen* to Scripture inwardly. Both mind and heart, study and prayer, are necessary to assimilate Scripture into

one's life. Indeed, knowing Scripture in this way unites one
with Christ, which is why *Dei Verbum* cites the famous dictum of St. Jerome, "Ignorance of the Scriptures is ignorance
of Christ."[20] *Dei Verbum* section 25 subsequently encourages
the lay faithful and religious to become familiar with Sacred
Scripture and then offers this exhortation:

> Let them remember that prayer should ac-
> company the reading of Sacred Scripture, so
> that God and man may talk together; for "we
> speak to Him when we pray; we hear Him
> when we read the divine saying."

Here, *Dei Verbum* explicitly urges the unity of Scripture study and prayer. Indeed, how else can "we hear Him
when we read the divine saying" unless we read and study
Scripture in such a way that our heart is also open to the
Lord in prayer at the same time.

Pastores Dabo Vobis also frequently encourages the
unity of exegesis and prayer, especially in section 47:

> An essential element of spiritual formation
> is the prayerful and meditated reading of the
> word of God (lectio divina), a humble and
> loving listening of him who speaks....
>
> A loving knowledge of the word of
> God and a prayerful familiarity with it are
> specifically important for the prophetic min-
> istry of the priest. They are a fundamental
> condition for such a ministry to be carried
> out suitably, especially if we bear in mind the
> "new evangelization" which the Church to-
> day is called to undertake.

Not only are exegesis and prayer to be integrated, but prayer itself is the appropriate response to Scripture study: "The first and fundamental manner of responding to the word is prayer, which is without any doubt a primary value and demand of spiritual formation."[21]

The Goal is Intimacy with Christ

Why integrate exegesis and prayer? Seminary formation is not just job training. "Formation is first and foremost cooperation with the grace of God."[22] Seminary study is not just a technical study of religion, but "intellectual formation in the seminary program centers on theology as a search for 'an ever deeper knowledge of the divine mysteries,'" as the *Program of Priestly Formation* section 163 reminds us. The unity of exegesis and prayer is to bring about in the priest a new outlook, the mind of Christ, as *Pastores Dabo Vobis* section 26 states:

[T]he priest himself ought first of all to develop a great personal familiarity with the word of God. Knowledge of its linguistic or exegetical aspects, though certainly necessary, is not enough. He needs to approach the word with a docile and prayerful heart so that it may deeply penetrate his thoughts and feelings and bring about a new outlook in him— "the mind of Christ" (1 Cor. 2:16)—such that his words and his choices and attitudes

> may become ever more a reflection, a procla-
> mation and a witness to the Gospel. Only if
> he "abides" in the word will the priest become
> a perfect disciple of the Lord.

The *Decree on the Ministry and Life of Priests (Presbyterorum Ordinis)* section 19 states, "The knowledge of the sacred minister ought to be sacred because it is drawn from the sacred source and directed to a sacred goal. Especially is it drawn from reading and meditating on the Sacred Scriptures."

Therefore, the Vatican II decree on priestly training, *Optatam Totius*, advises that seminarians "should be taught to seek Christ in the faithful meditation on God's word."[23] Once again, we see that the integration of Scripture study and prayer is what the council seeks in priestly formation, and the goal of this integration is that the seminarian develops intimacy with Christ, "to seek Christ."

Likewise, *Pastores Dabo Vobis* section 45 recommends, "They should be taught to seek Christ in faithful meditation on the word of God." The goal of seminary training is, therefore, not just to graduate with a theological degree but to come to know Christ. Hence *Pastores Dabo Vobis* section 46 states, "Those who are to take on the likeness of Christ the priest by sacred ordination should form the habit of drawing close to him as friends in every detail of their lives"; and *Pastores Dabo Vobis* section 57 recommends, "The whole formation imparted to candidates for the priesthood aims at preparing them to enter into communion with the charity of Christ the good shepherd."

Naturally, the friendship a seminarian develops with Christ while in seminary will continue to grow after receiving Holy Orders. Therefore *Pastores Dabo Vobis* section 46 states:

> So inexhaustible is the mystery of the imitation of Christ and the sharing in his life that this "seeking" will also have to continue throughout the priest's life and ministry. Likewise this "finding" the Master will have to continue in order to bring him to others, or rather in order to excite in others the desire to seek out the Master.

When a seminarian experiences theology as encounter with God, naturally, he will want to continue to grow in his theological study after ordination and, through it, grow in his encountering God. "Theology may be legitimately approached as a way toward intimate familiarity with God, rather than it being simply an academic seeking to articulate ideas about God."[24] *Pastores Dabo Vobis* emphasizes the seminarian's call to divine intimacy: "the priest needs to be trained to have a deep intimacy with God. Those who are preparing for the priesthood should realize that their whole priestly life will have value inasmuch as they are able to give themselves to Christ and through Christ to the Father;"[25] and again, "The priestly vocation is essentially a call to holiness in the form which derives from the sacrament of orders. Holiness is intimacy with God."[26] Priesthood and prayer, as well as religious life and prayer, are intrinsically united as *Novo Millennio Ineunte* section 34 states:

> Christians who have received the gift of a vocation to the specially consecrated life are of course called to prayer in a particular way:

of its nature, their consecration makes them more open to the experience of contemplation, and it is important that they should cultivate it with special care.

In fact, one cannot be missionary without intimacy with Christ because "an essential characteristic of missionary spirituality is intimate communion with Christ."[27]

Parishes Intimate with Christ

The *Program of Priestly Formation* reminds us that Scripture study in seminary is directed to a pastoral end, "the preparation of seminarians for the tasks of preaching homilies and applying Scripture to the lives of the Christian faithful."[28] Therefore, we can say that the ultimate goal of this approach to priestly formation is not just a priest intimately united with Christ but a parish brought to intimacy with Christ through its pastor because its pastor is intimate with Christ. Thus, Pope John Paul II said to the Austrian bishops, "The first question we can be asked as Pastors is not: 'What have you organized?' but: 'Whom have you led to communion with the Triune God?'"[29] *Presbyterorum Ordinis* section 5 states:

> Priests likewise must instruct their people to participate in the celebrations of the sacred liturgy in such a way that they become proficient in genuine prayer. They must coax their people on to an ever more perfect

and constant spirit of prayer for every grace and need.

The *Directory on the Ministry and Life of Priests* by the Congregation for the Clergy section 36 states, "In recent years, in effect, it has become evident that there is an eminently pastoral necessity for the priest to be a man of God and a *teacher of prayer*" (emphasis mine).

We can say, therefore, that as well as being faithful to literary critical methods, spirituality supplies the seminary professor and his teaching with a fuller methodology for teaching. The origin and power of this fuller methodology is Christ; and reading, studying, and praying Scripture with Christ results in priests and parishes intimate with Christ.

Practical Applications

We offer some suggestions here that may prove helpful to a seminary Scripture professor. Since professors are already familiar with applying the historical-critical method and synchronic methods for many years before becoming professors, I will concentrate here on practical ways to apply the desire for integration of exegesis and prayer. This is not in any way taking away from applying literary critical methods to Scripture study but simply adding another layer of meaning to our understanding of Scripture, just as synchronic methods add more layers of meaning to the historical-critical method.

Naturally, we cannot give what we do not first have ourselves, and an intimate relationship with Christ is a prerequisite for the seminary professor in any discipline. Our theology is to flow from our prayer, and our theology leads us to prayer.

This leads us to commence each class with prayer and conclude each class with prayer, so that in a real sense, our theology does indeed flow from prayer and lead us to prayer. Ideally, the opening class prayer should lead us into the theology under exploration in our class, and the closing class prayer would be our prayerful response to what we covered in class.

It would be helpful to pause for a brief moment of silence when appropriate and ask the seminarians to reflect on what the Lord is saying to them through this scriptural exegesis or theological study. The final moments of class naturally lend themselves to this reflection, but some class content may lend itself to these brief reflective moments at other times during the class. Students have given positive feedback for integrating these reflective moments into class. We are already accustomed to such silences after the homily and after receiving Holy Communion, so this use of silence is not groundbreaking. If we introduce these brief reflective moments into class, we can also insert a goal/objective in our syllabi that the students integrate their academic study of Scripture into their spirituality.

As professors, we can continually ask ourselves questions to help us discern how we can teach in way that integrates knowledge and relationship with Christ: "How is this class helping seminarians to receive the love of Christ?";

"How is this class fascinating seminarians with God?"; "How does this class help seminarians encounter God?"; "How does this class help seminarians become more intimate with Christ?"

Some students who have spent a summer at The Institute for Priestly Formation are accustomed not only to taking academic notes but also including in their notes what the Lord is saying to them through this study. An introductory course on Scripture could include some instruction and praxis on lectio divina, and seminaries naturally lend themselves to giving Scripture professors other opportunities to help seminarians contemplate the Lord in the Scriptures.

These are but humble suggestions, but hopefully, seminary Scripture professors can be original in developing many other ways of accomplishing the stipulations of the *Program of Priestly Formation* to teach seminarians a methodology to exegete Scripture using literary critical methods integrated with prayer to arrive at intimacy with Christ.

Notes

1   United States Conference of Catholic Bishops, *Program of Priestly Formation*, 5th ed. (Washington, DC: USCCB, 2006).

2   Ibid., 200.

3   Ibid.

4   Pontifical Biblical Commission, *The Interpretation of the Bible in the Church* (Vatican City: Libreria Editrice Vaticana, 1993), 18.

5   A history of the involvement of the Catholic Church in the historical-critical method may be found in the doctoral dissertation of Prior, Joseph G. *The Historical Critical Method in Catholic Exegesis* Tesi gregoriana, Serie teologia, no. 50 (Rome: Editrice Pontificio Università Gregoriana, 1999), 89.

6   Pontifical Biblical Commission, *Sancta Mater Ecclesia* (1964), 6.

7   Williamson, Peter S., *Catholic Principles for Interpreting Scripture: A Study of the Pontifical Biblical Commission's* The Interpretation of the Bible in the Church, Subsidia Biblica, no. 22 (Rome: Editrice Pontificio Istituto Biblico, 2001) identifies and explains twenty key principles of Catholic biblical interpretation in *The Interpretation of the Bible in the Church*. Available for digital download from logos.com. A summary by Williamson is in "Catholic Principles for Interpreting Scripture" *CBQ* 65 (2003): 327-349.

8   Ibid., secs. 27-29, 11.

9   Pope Benedict XVI, *Faith, Reason and the University: Memories and Reflections*, Address during the Meeting with the Representatives of Science at the University of Regensburg, (September 12, 2006) http://www.vatican.va/holy_father/benedict_xvi/speeches/2006/september/documents/hf_ben-xvi_spe_20060912_university-regensburg_en.html

10   Congregation for Catholic Education, *Instruction on the Study of the Fathers of the Church in the Formation of Priests*, my translation, (November 10, 1989), http://www.vatican.va/roman_curia/congregations/ccatheduc/documents/rc_con_ccatheduc_doc_19891110_padri_it.html

11   Ibid., 26.1.

12   Ibid.

13   Ibid., 40.4

14   Pieper, Josef, *Guide to Thomas Aquinas* trans. Richard and Clara Winston (New York: Pantheon Books, 1962), 120-121.

15   Second Vatican Council, *Dei Verbum* (1965), 11.

16   *Program of Priestly Formation*, 200.

17   Ibid.

18   Ibid., 115.

19 Ibid., 163.
20 St. Jerome, Commentary on Isaiah, Prol.: PL 24,17.
21 John Paul II, *Pastores Dabo Vobis* (1992), 47.
22 Ibid., 68.
23 Documents of Vatican II, *Optatam Totius* (1965), 8.
24 James Keating, *Resting on the Heart of Christ: The Vocation and Spirituality of the Seminary Theologian* (Omaha: IPF Publications, 2009), 63.
25 *Pastores Dabo Vobis*, 47.
26 Ibid., 33.
27 John Paul II, *Redemptoris Missio* (1990), 88.
28 *Program of Priestly Formation*, 200.
29 Pope John Paul II, *Address to Bishops of Austria on their "Ad Limina Apostolorum" Visit*, (November 20, 1998), http://www.vatican.va/holy_father/john_paul_ii/speeches/1998/november/documents/hf_jp-ii_spe_19981120_ad-limina-austria_en.html

Lecture Divina

The Fathers of the Church and Theological Pedagogy

Perry Cahall, PhD

Introduction

The title of this essay is clearly a play on words. It came from the initial suggestion of James Keating that I consider crafting an essay focusing on the history of *lectio divina* and its contribution to today's seminary classroom. As I began to tackle this project, a couple of things happened. First, it became clear to me how *lectio divina* must influence today's seminary classroom. Anyone teaching theology is called to spend time prayerfully reading Sacred Scripture if Scripture really is to be the heart and soul of their theologizing.[1] Second, *lectio* will influence the classroom to the extent that the students themselves undertake the practice, bringing Spirit-guided insights into the dynamics of the classroom conversation. However, incorporating the practice of *lectio divina* into *classroom time* in any regular fashion is hard to envision. Nonetheless, it was immediately apparent to me that the goal of *lectio*, "to truly enter, by means of the word, into contact with the Word of God,"[2] should, without a doubt, be part of seminary teaching. In fact, to enable others to encounter Christ through the words of his teaching should be the goal of any theologian worthy of the title. Pope Benedict XVI said as much when he said of the theologian: "This is his mission: in the talkativeness of our time and of other times, in the inflation of words, to make the essential words present. In words make the Word present, the Word that proceeds from God, the Word that is God."[3] It is in this way that I began to consider the task of teaching theology as "lecture *divina*," a prayerful and contemplative approach to teaching with the goal of enabling others to encounter Christ.

With this last point in mind, my thoughts started drifting toward the Fathers of the Church. First of all, it occurred to me that the Fathers all practiced *lectio divina* in some form and that they constantly urged others to live with and in the Scriptures in order to grow in intimacy with Christ. "For the Fathers, Sacred Scripture was the object of unconditioned veneration, the foundation of the faith, the constant subject of preaching, nourishment of devotion, the soul of theology."[4] After all, who can forget St. Jerome's famous dictum, "Ignorance of the Scriptures is ignorance of Christ."[5] Yet, as I allowed my thoughts to drift toward the Fathers, it also occurred to me that the Fathers serve as more than just models of how to incorporate *lectio divina* into the teaching of theology. More broadly, with their great love for wisdom and their desire to communicate it, the Fathers serve as sapiential models for teaching theology. Certainly there have been such teachers in every age of the Church, but the earliest centuries of Christianity hold examples of some of the greatest teachers and writers of all time, who integrated their intellectual and spiritual lives in a preeminent manner to address various pastoral and human concerns. They clearly saw how "intellectual formation contributes to spiritual formation ... [serving] to deepen one's spiritual journey,"[6] and they saw the spiritual life as "the center around which all other aspects [of Christian formation] are integrated."[7] Therefore, seminary theologians can look to the Church Fathers as model practitioners of their craft.

For the past several years, I have had the privilege of teaching a Patristics course in the seminary. This is both one of the most challenging and one of the easiest courses that I have ever taught. It is challenging because of the responsibility that I have of choosing course readings that will allow the students to meaningfully navigate the rich heritage bequeathed to us by the early Church Fathers. Making these choices is extremely difficult, and I am constantly rethinking my choices, revising the syllabus from year to year, and relying on student feedback to improve students' experience of the course. However, teaching this course is also easy because, with very few exceptions, no matter what Patristic texts I choose, the students are impressed by the writings of the Fathers. They are impressed not only by the intellectual insights of these theological giants, but as much, and sometimes more so, by the liveliness and passion with which the Fathers write. The seminarians are taken by the Fathers' pastoral zeal and by how practical and applicable their theological insights are, over fifteen hundred years later. Most of all, seminarians are enthralled by the love with which the Fathers write and how their single-minded goal is to enable others to participate in the life of God by bringing them into contact with Jesus Christ. The Fathers clearly sought "to live in intimate and unceasing union with God the Father through his Son, Jesus Christ, in the Holy Spirit ... [in] communion with the Church."[8] While it is not possible to treat the theology of the Church Fathers as a monolithic entity, in what follows I will outline several common qualities of the theology of the Church Fathers, aspects of a manner of teaching, that allow current seminary theologians to look to the Church Fathers as sapiential models of teaching.

The Centrality of Love for the Theologian

The Church Fathers showed that theology is, by its very nature, relational. They saw that, "there can be no knowledge of God without a relation between the knower and God."[9] St. Athanasius of Alexandria articulated that the Word "comes in condescension to show loving-kindness to us, and to visit us."[10] Starting with their reflection on God's loving initiative, the Fathers themselves fell deeply in love and allowed themselves to be transformed by the Love whom they encountered. Above all else, the Church Fathers "were specialists in the supernatural life who communicated what they had seen and experienced in their contemplation of divine things, what they had known through the path of love."[11] The Fathers had "a great familiarity with God, a lived experience of the mystery of Christ and the Church."[12] In their work, "the Fathers certainly appreciated the usefulness of speculation, but they knew it was not enough. In the same intellectual effort to understand their own faith, they practiced love that ... became by its very nature the source of new understanding."[13] For the Church Fathers, "The goal was not only understanding but love,"[14] because love brings with it a new mode of understanding. St. Augustine highlighted the primacy of love by noting, "when there is a question of whether a man is good, one does not ask what he believes, or what he hopes, but what he loves. For the man who loves aright no doubt believes and hopes aright."[15]

Perhaps Robert Wilken makes the point best when he states, "The church gave men and women a new love, Jesus Christ, a person who inspired their actions and held their affections. This was a love unlike others."[16] The Church Fathers poured themselves out in service to this love. "They wished not only to understand and express the dazzling truth they had seen in Christ, [but] by thinking and writing they sought to know God more intimately and love him more ardently."[17] They realized that the more they grew in knowledge of Christ, the more they could grow in love of Christ. As Augustine said, "It is quite certain that nothing can be loved unless it is known."[18] This is why he and the other Church Fathers sought to understand and articulate their faith in Christ and His relationship to the Father in the communion of Love that is the Trinity.[19] "Everything in their pastoral action and teaching is brought back to charity, and charity to Christ, the universal way of salvation."[20]

Robert Wilken has noted, "Nothing is more characteristic of the Christian intellectual tradition than its fondness for the language of the heart."[21] Today's teachers of theology in the seminary must not shy away from this language. They must be deeply in love with the object of their study, the way the Church Fathers were, if they are to succeed in fostering a love for theology in seminarians. To be effective in any discipline, teachers must be in love with their subject matter; however, for the theologian, this is true in a unique way, for the subject matter of theology is the living God who has revealed Himself fully and definitively in the Person of Jesus Christ.

Hence, the subject theologians teach and the object of their research and study is a Person, and this Person seeks a relationship of love with the theologian. This Person knows the theologian better than the theologian knows himself and better than the theologian can ever know the object of his study. The Personal object of the theologian's study wishes that what the theologian can know about Him through his intellectual efforts will serve to draw the theologian deeper into the Mystery of Love who is the Trinity. And further, this Love wishes that the theologian extend to others through his intellectual work the invitation to enter this Love. This is exactly what the Church Fathers did. For example, in writing about the Trinity, Augustine exhorted his readers to love and at the same time, invited them into the Mystery of Love when he said, "if a man is full of love, what is he full of but God?"[22]

The seminary theologian, emulating the Church Fathers, must invest himself in his study and teaching in a manner that is not required of practitioners of other disciplines. Hans Urs Van Balthasar noted, "one does not guide someone into love in the same way he introduces a theoretical science, rather, he introduces someone to love by permitting him to participate in love's reality, by teaching him to love within the all-encompassing love of God."[23] Unlike other academics, the theologian must constantly challenge himself to be vulnerable to the object of his study. "For the knowledge that brings happiness is ours only in love,"[24] and love makes demands. Love requires a personal commitment on the part of the lover and a willingness to sacrifice for the beloved. As Robert Wilken has beautifully stated:

> Unless we invest ourselves in the object of our love, we remain voyeurs and spectators, curiosity seekers, incapable of receiving because we are unwilling to give...Only when we turn our deepest self to God can we enter the mystery of God's life and penetrate the truth of things. If love is absent, our minds remain childish and immature, trying out one thing and then another, unable to hold fast to the truth.[25]

Seminarians must see in their professors a loving devotion to the object of theology that is both committed and vulnerable if they are to live out this same dynamic with Christ and His people.

The Church Fathers were mature Christian thinkers because they clearly saw that, "only when wounded by

love can one know the God of the Bible."[26] They opened
their hearts to God and, thus, allowed God to reveal their
hearts to themselves. This is never more clear than in the
oration delivered by St. Ambrose of Milan on the occasion
of his brother's funeral. In this incredibly moving piece, St.
Ambrose lays his heart bare before God and his congregation. He is a man stricken with grief who places his wounded
heart before God. He admits to his congregation, "Nothing
among things of earth, dearest brethren, was more precious
to me, nothing more worthy of love, nothing more dear than
such a brother,"[27] for whom he admits to shedding many tears
of grief.[28] Yet, because of the "great mystery of divine love"
by which the Father did not except His own Son from death
for us, Ambrose knows "that divine love could not die."[29] It is
this knowledge that allows him to offer "that [his] grief may
be a ransom for the grief of all."[30] This self-oblation of love,
in imitation of the self-offering of Jesus, was only possible
because this preeminent pastor and theologian allowed himself to be vulnerable to the object of his study. This vulnerability allowed him simultaneously to be vulnerable to his
congregation and offer them a lesson in love that they surely
did not soon forget. Seminary professors, through the love
that is at the heart of their vocation, must enable the future
priests whom they are teaching to offer similar lessons.

Theology Cannot Be Only an Intellectual Exercise

Since their goal was to lead others into the Love of
God, for the Fathers, the craft of theology was much more

than just an intellectual pursuit. As Robert Wilken has noted: "The intellectual effort of the early church was at the service of a much loftier goal than giving conceptual form to Christian belief. Its mission was to win the hearts and minds of men and women and to change their lives."[31] This must be the same mission of the seminary theologian. For the Fathers, theology was not an exercise in esoteric thinking hovering in the stratosphere of abstract and theoretical concepts. On the contrary, everything the Fathers taught had the clear and concrete goal of drawing others into the love of God through Jesus Christ. St. Gregory Nazianzen made the point that the whole reason for the Word to unite his higher divine nature to an inferior human nature was "in order that [man] too might be made God so far as He is made Man."[32] This was the concrete realization to which the Fathers wanted to bring everyone.

It is worth bearing in mind that the Church Fathers were "doing theology" long before theology became a professional academic discipline. The Fathers did not hold tenure track positions, were not operating under the "publish or perish" mentality, and were not worried about the renewal of their contracts. When they wrote, they did so not to fulfill any professional requirements nor to prove to others how bright they were, but only because they felt the need to lead others to the life-changing Truth who is Jesus Christ. "There was no intellectual elitism among the church fathers."[33] As theologians, they did not try to set themselves apart as a group of scholars possessing some kind of special knowledge or insights that the common Christians did not have. In fact, they roundly condemned such elitism. St. Irenaeus of Lyons spent the majority of his adult life combating such smugness in his refutation of the Gnostics, whose belief system was elitist. Against the Gnostics who claimed to have a secret knowledge that alone could grant access to salvation, Irenaeus said, "Each one of them is wholly perverse, and is not ashamed to preach himself, corrupting the rule of faith."[34] He noted that "the Lord imparted knowledge of the truth to his disciples ... [H]e did not speak to them in accordance with their previous ideas, nor answer in accordance with the presumptions of inquirers, but in accordance with the sound teaching, without any pretense or respect for persons."[35]

Instead of being a realm of secret knowledge involving esoteric concepts and theories accessible to only a few, the Fathers' theology was for everyone, and it appealed to more than just the intellect. In his allocution for the inauguration of the "Augustinianum" Patristics Institute, Pope Paul VI noted that the Fathers spoke, "not only to the intellect, but to the whole person involving thought, will and feeling."[36] For the Fathers, theology was not only about informing minds, but about transforming persons. St. Cyril of Jerusalem made this abundantly clear when he reminded the newly baptized, "Having been baptized into Christ, and put on Christ, you have been made conformable to the Son of God...[and] are properly called Christs."[37] Similarly, St. Gregory Nazianzen made the argument that the Word had to have assumed a human mind, because if He had not, then He could not have healed it and helped us to avoid sin.[38] The Fathers did not treat God as an object of rational enquiry but as the Mystery whom one must enter if one is to experience personal transformation that leads to true fulfillment and lasting happiness.[39] They desperately desired others to experience the transformative power of the Gospel. For as Athanasius said, the Son of God "was made man so that we might be made God."[40]

In all of their theologizing, the Fathers make it very clear that the goal of theology is not simply an increase of knowledge or a mastery of difficult concepts. The Fathers' "intellectual work was always in service of praise and adoration of the one God."[41] They sought to understand the object of their study, namely God, so that they could enter more deeply into prayerful communion with the Divine. Who can forget Augustine's longing cry, "Our hearts are restless, Oh God, until they rest in you."[42] In this way, the Fathers show that doctrine is never dry and not merely a matter of academic precision. On the contrary, the Fathers always showed how rectitude of doctrine was connected to daily life. Seminary professors must do the same if they hope to engender in the seminarians a life-long love of learning that they should see as indispensable for guiding the daily lives of their parishioners. For the Church Fathers, "Life and doctrine are immediately one."[43] St. Gregory of Nyssa wrote, "all ... gifts are wrought in those who are worthy alike by the Father, the Son, and the Holy Spirit: every grace and power, guidance, life, comfort, the change to immortality, the passage to liberty, and every other boon that exists, which descends to us."[44] Thus, Gregory, and all the Fathers, show that what one believes dictates how one lives. He shows that to think correctly about God and to understand something of His Mystery enables one to enter more deeply into the life and love of the Trinity and, thus, fulfill the meaning of our existence beginning in the here and now—hardly a mere academic exercise.

Relating Everything to Jesus

Since Jesus alone provides the way to the Father, the goal theology aims to accomplish is only possible to the extent that the theologian enables his students to encounter the Word made flesh. Robert Wilken summarizes the Fathers' approach to theology well when he states, "Theory was not an end in itself, and concepts and abstractions were always put at the service of a deeper immersion in the *res*, the thing itself, the mystery of Christ and the practice of the Christian life."[45] Hence, bringing others into contact with the life-changing message of the Gospel brought by Jesus Christ is the simple and overarching goal of all of the Fathers' teaching efforts. To be clear, the Fathers provide deep and profound reflections on and explanations of the Gospel message, but the heart of all of their reflections is Jesus. Even though the Fathers understood that Jesus is the definitive starting point for understanding reality, they also understood Jesus is not the answer to a riddle nor the conclusion to an argument. They understood Jesus not so much as a solution to a problem or Himself a problem to be solved, but a Mystery to be encountered through the Church and a Mystery to be lived with and lived in.

The teaching of the Fathers

> is entirely centered on the mystery of Christ to whom all the individual truths are referred in a wonderful synthesis.... the Fathers look at the whole in its center and make this whole present in each of its parts...Following the Fathers in their theological itinerary means,

therefore, grasping more easily the essential nucleus of our faith and the 'specificum' of our Christian identity.[46]

No matter what topic they addressed, the Fathers related everything back to Jesus. By their example, they show the seminary theologian that not only must he make connections among the truths of the faith, but he must ultimately show how everything is connected to Jesus who, as the Light of the world, sheds light on everything, and as the Truth who demands that everything be viewed in His light. As St. Justin Martyr pointed out, it was "reason himself, who took form and became man and was called Jesus Christ."[47] This fact must change how we reason about everything.

The Church Fathers saw Sacred Scripture as a book which was, from beginning to end, about Christ. As they saw all of reality through the lens of Jesus, so also they did not hesitate to read all of Scripture through the same lens. For the Fathers, there was no one theory or hermeneutical approach that promised to unlock the meaning of the Bible. For them the key to Scripture was the Person of Jesus Christ. They saw that Jesus is God's definitive Word, the fullness of revelation, and that all the words of Scripture must be viewed with respect to Him. St. Ignatius of Antioch testified to this clearly when he wrote, "To my mind it is Jesus Christ who is the original document."[48]

Robert Wilken has noted that from the birth of Christian theology, one of its most distinctive features was that it reasoned *from* Christ and not *to* Him.[49] Now that Reason had become man, the approach to understanding reality had to change. No longer was God "the conclusion of an argument, the end of a search for an ultimate explanation" as was the case for the Greek philosophers.[50] Now man had seen the face of God, and this revelation changed everything. Knowing God was no longer a matter of intellectual abstraction, but instead, a matter of personal encounter with the Word become Flesh. The Fathers taught that "reason can no longer be exercised independently of what has happened in Christ and, it must be added, came to be because of Christ."[51] The Fathers understood that with Christ, we now have our definitive starting point for understanding all of reality. By their example, the Fathers teach seminary theologians that they should strive to lead their students into this new approach to reality. The seminary theologian must relate everything to Jesus, or rather, show how Jesus gives everything its definitive meaning. By doing this, he will deepen the seminarian's intimacy with Christ and show him how indispensable theology is to his call to be *in persona Christi*. If the theologian does not seek to relate everything to Jesus, then he really cannot call himself a theologian. St. Hilary of Poitiers pointed to this concept when he wrote,

> We hold it right to remind the members of our common faith, that the knowledge of the Eternal is presented in the same confession which gives eternal life. He does not, he cannot know his own life, who is ignorant that Christ Jesus was very God, as He was very man.[52]

Encountering Christ, the God-man, must be the goal to which the theologian leads his students, so that they may experience His love and, thereby, know their own lives.

The Theologian as Student of the Church

With profound humility, the Fathers understood that one cannot truly encounter Christ without the Church. "It can be said that this attitude of respect and humility is none other than lively awareness of the insuperable limits that the human intellect experiences in the face of divine transcendence."[53] The Fathers understood intuitively that theology is a dependent discipline—completely dependent upon what the transcendent God has revealed of Himself. They understood that God is ineffable Mystery and that we could know nothing about Him on our own efforts. They also understood that God has freely chosen to reveal Himself through Creation, in human history, through the words of Sacred Scripture, and most fully, in the Person of Jesus Christ. They further realized that the safeguarding of this revelation has been entrusted by Christ to the Church and that they continually encountered Christ through the faith and the worship life of the Church. St. Irenaeus of Lyons stressed that the Church has preserved and transmitted the faith and safeguards the "rule of faith."[54] St. Cyprian of Carthage made this point forcefully when he said, "He can no longer have God for his Father, who has not the Church for his mother,"[55] and St. Clement of Rome made the same point when he wrote, "They cannot dwell with God who would not be of one mind in God's Church."[56] Thus, it is not an overstatement to say that for the Fathers "there was no Christian thinking without the church."[57]

The Fathers clearly embodied the phrase *sentire cum ecclesia* (to think with the Church) and they teach others to do the same. In a letter to them, Clement of Rome exhorted the Corinthians to "turn to the glorious and holy rule of our tradition"[58] and throughout the same letter, there are constant exhortations not to harm the unity of the Church. For the Fathers, "Faithfulness, not originality, was the mark of a good teacher."[59] This is not to say that the Fathers did not take chances in expressing the truth or that they lacked daring in trying to delve into and articulate divine Mysteries. However, it does mean that even in the daring chances that they took, they always sought to work within the faith of the Church.

This needs to be the same for today's teachers of theology in seminaries. The seminary theologian should not see himself as an innovator and should not thrive on being on the cutting edge of his field, titillating his students with novel ideas. Instead, he should follow the model of the Church Fathers and teach his students to do the same. He should show the seminarians that far from being a shackle to creativity or a barrier to intellectual freedom, the teaching and life of the Church truly liberates one to pursue truth in creative and daring ways. As Robert Wilken has noted, "The church fathers wrote 'as those who are taught'" (Is 50:4).[60] Likewise, today's seminary professor must teach as one who is taught.

The fact that the Church Fathers saw themselves as students of the Church is evident in how they used Scripture. Robert Wilken has noted,

> In contrast to modern theological writings in which the Bible is cited in support of theological ideas, and hence usually relegated to

the footnotes, in the early church the words of the Bible were the linguistic skeleton for the exposition of ideas. Even in the writings of the most philosophical of early Christian thinkers their thoughts are expressed in the language of the Bible, seldom above it.[61]

Yet, Wilken has also noted, "The liturgy provided a kind of grammar of Christian speech, a key to how the words of the Bible are to be used."[62] Thus it was the Church's worship life that provided the Church Fathers with a Biblical lexicon. By allowing themselves to be taught by the Liturgy, the Church Fathers knew how to approach the Biblical text. Hence it is accurate to say that the Church Fathers

> did not consider themselves masters but servants of the Sacred Scriptures since they [the Church Fathers] had received them [Sacred Scriptures] from the Church, read and commented on them in and for the Church, according to the rule of faith proposed and illustrated by ecclesiastical and apostolic Tradition.[63]

As Augustine noted, "But I would not believe in the Gospel, had not the authority of the Catholic Church already moved me."[64]

The Church's "rule of faith" guided how the Church Fathers read the Scriptures. And, this rule of faith was experienced in the life of the Church. All of the Fathers' "thinking was never far removed from the church's worship."[65] As Robert Wilken has noted,

> By constant immersion in the *res liturgicae*
> early Christian thinkers came face to face
> with the living Christ and could say with
> Thomas the apostle, 'My Lord and God.' Here
> was a truth so tangible, so enduring, so com-
> pelling that it trumped every religious idea.
> Understanding was achieved not by stepping
> back and viewing things from a distance but
> by entering into the revealed object itself.[66]

What the Fathers, "taught had to do not only with words
and ideas but palpable realities."[67]

> Before there were treatises on the Trinity,
> before there were learned commentaries on
> the Bible, before there were disputes about
> the teaching on grace, or essays on the moral
> life, there was awe and adoration before the
> exalted Son of God alive and present in the
> church's offering of the Eucharist. This truth
> preceded every effort to understand and
> nourished every attempt to express in words
> and concepts what Christians believed.[68]

St. Ignatius of Antioch encouraged the Ephesians to,
"try to gather more frequently to celebrate God's Eucharist
and praise him,"[69] and St. Cyril of Jerusalem exhorted,

> with full assurance let us partake of the
> Body and Blood of Christ: for in the figure
> of Bread is given to thee His Body, and in
> the figure of Wine His Blood; that thou by
> partaking of the Body and Blood of Christ,
> may be made of the same body and the same
> blood with Him.[70]

Emulating the Church Fathers, seminary theology today must develop "in intimate connection with the church's life, her sacraments and practices, Scripture and creeds, martyrs and saints, and in the company of the whole host of heaven."[71] The teacher of theology should always remember that

> theology was born out of the exegetic activity of the Fathers, 'in medio Ecclesiae,' and especially in the liturgical assemblies in contact with the spiritual needs of the People of God. That exegesis in which spiritual life is blended with rational theological reflection always aims at the essentials, while being faithful to the entire sacred deposit of the faith.[72]

As he seeks to be faithful to this deposit and prior to standing before his students, the seminary theologian must experience the Lord in the heart of the Church—reading Scripture with the mind of the Church in accord with the faith of the saints, encountering the Risen Lord in the Sacraments, and kneeling before him in humble adoration. He must be immersed in the Church's Liturgy, praying with the Church, so that he can seek to extend the Liturgy into the classroom. The theologian would do well to follow St. Cyril of Jerusalem's counsel to "give thanks unto God, who has accounted you worthy of so great mysteries."[73] He would also do well to follow the example of Augustine, who at the end of his work on the Trinity wrote, "let us bring this book to a close at last with a prayer in preference to an argument."[74] There is a great deal of truth in saying that good theology begins and ends on one's knees.

Seminary Theologian as Witness

Robert Wilken has rightly noted "the omnipresence of the Bible in early Christian writings."[75] He has noted how the Bible shaped the way the Church Fathers thought about reality and how their theology is articulated primarily through biblical themes, stories, and images. Moreover, Wilken also notes that, "the Word of God makes its way not by argument but as men and women bear witness to what has happened."[76] This is the Biblical mode that was adopted by the Church Fathers and that should be adopted by the seminary theologian. In their teaching, the Church Fathers bore witness to the love that transformed their intellects and changed their lives, and the seminary professor must do the same. If the professor has allowed himself to be transformed by love, then he cannot but be a witness. If he is a witness, then he will enable the future priests seated in class in front of him to be the same.

To understand the importance of his witness, the seminary teacher should remember that

> God...is known primarily through events that take place in history...Accordingly, the way to God begins not with arguments or proofs but with discernment and faith, the ability to see what is disclosed in events and the readiness to trust the words of those who testify to them.[77]

While the effective teacher of theology has to present cogent arguments, he must also enable his students to recognize God in the events of their lives, just as some day, the seminarians will be assisting their parishioners to recognize God in the events of their lives. The seminary professor can develop this vision only by gaining the seminarians' trust through his personal witness to the truth of the Gospel and its effect on his life. Taking the Church Fathers as their models, teachers of theology in seminaries must teach as much or more by their lives than by their eloquent words.

All the Church Fathers show that "the place to begin is not with the truth or falsity of certain teachings, but with the persons whose lives are formed by the teachings."[78] They show that coming to the truth is "about placing one's confidence in men and women whose examples invite us to love what they love."[79] They placed their confidence in the witness of the apostles, who were willing to die for the love of Christ, and the Church Fathers, in turn, were willing to do the same. Even though the teacher of theology might not have the opportunity to witness to Christ unto his own death, he must witness to the transforming power of Christ's love in the integrity of his life, being willing to die for Christ. Without this example, his words will mean very little.

Conclusion

For the Church Fathers, the craft of theology was more than a mere intellectual exercise. For them, "The intellectual task was a spiritual undertaking"[80] at the service of love. In reading the Fathers, one gets the sense that they would counsel the seminary theologian that if he is not teaching others how to better love and serve God and, thus, how to attain eternal union with Him, then he is not really teaching anything at all. The Fathers never approached theology as a subject to be dissected and studied, but instead approached theology as a loving conversation with God. They taught with love what they learned from this conversation. Jesus was always at the center of all of their reflections, and for them, there was no dichotomy between Jesus and the Church. In fact, they came to know Jesus only through their participation in the life of the Church. It was in being faithful students of the Church that the Fathers had continual access to the Love that was at the center of all of their efforts and that fanned the flame of their own love. By the witness of their lives transformed by the love of Christ, the Fathers taught that "the goal of human life is not to know something about God, but to know God and be known by God, to delight in the face of God."[81] The desire to grow in this knowledge that leads to love must be the heart of the sapiential and contemplative way of teaching theology and in this craft, the Church Fathers "are still our teachers today."[82]

Notes

1   See Second Vatican Council, *Dei Verbum* (1965), sec. 11; United States Catholic Conference, *Catechism of the Catholic Church* (Washington, DC: USCC Publishing, 1997, 2nd Edition), sec. 132.

2   Mario Masini, *Lectio Divina: An Ancient Prayer That Is Ever New*, trans. Edmund C. Lane (New York: Alba House, 1998), 6.

3   Benedict XVI, Homily to members of the International Theological Commission (Oct. 6, 2006) <http://www.zenit.org/article-17840?l=english>

4   Congregation for Catholic Education, *Instruction on the Study of the Fathers of the Church in the Formation of Priests* (Washington, D.C.: USCCB Publishing, 1989), 26.2.

5   Cited in *Catechism of the Catholic Church* (CCC) 133, (Washington, DC: USCCB Publishing, 2000).

6   United States Conference of Catholic Bishops, *Program of Priestly Formation*, 5th edition (Washington, DC: USCCB, 2006), 113.

7   Ibid., 115.

8   Ibid., 108.

9   Robert Louis Wilken, *The Spirit of Early Christian Thought: Seeking the Face of God* (New Haven: Yale University Press, 2003), 21. I cannot recommend this book highly enough as a wonderful introduction to the thought world of the early Church Fathers, attempting to show "how Christians thought about the things they believed" (xiv). This book represents insights from a devoted scholar of the early Church who has spent a lifetime becoming familiar with the Fathers. In the Patristics course I teach, the seminarians have found this book incredibly helpful in coming to understand the theology of the Church Fathers. This present essay will rely heavily on some of Dr. Wilken's insights and observations.

10   Athanasius of Alexandria, *On the Incarnation of the Word*, trans. Archibald Robertson, Nicene and Post-Nicene Fathers, Second Series, Vol. 4. ed. Philip Schaff and Henry Wace (Buffalo, NY: Christian Literature Publishing Co., 1892), 8. This citation has been slightly modified by the author for readability.

11   *Instruction*, 39.

12   Ibid.

13   Ibid.

14   Wilken, xviii.

15   Augustine, *Enchiridion on Faith, Hope, and Love*, translated by J. B. Shaw (Washington, D.C.: Regnery Publishing, 1996), CXVII.

16   Wilken, xv.

17   Ibid., 26.

18   Augustine, *The Trinity*, trans. Edmund Hill, The Works of Saint Augustine: A translation for the 21st Century, I.5 (Brooklyn: New City Press, 1991), X.1.2.

19   See Ibid., VI, 17.

20   *Instruction*, 46.

21   Wilken, 292.

22   Augustine, *The Trinity*, VIII.5.12.

23   Hans Urs Van Balthasar, *Light of the Word: Brief Reflections on the Sunday Readings*, trans. Dennis D. Martin (San Francisco: Ignatius Press, 1993), 199.

24   Wilken, 292.

25   Ibid., 293.

26   Ibid., 7.

27   Ambrose, *On the Decease of His Brother Satyrus*, trans. H. de Romestin, E. de Romestin and H.T.F. Duckworth, NPNF, Second Series, Vol. 10 (Buffalo, NY: Christian Literature Publishing Co., 1896.), 2.

28   Ibid., 10.

29   Ibid., 4.

30   Ibid., 1.

31   Wilken, xiv.

32   Gregory Nazianzen, *The Third Theological Oration*, trans. Charles Gordon Browne and James Edward Swallow, NPNF, Second Series, Vol. 7 (Buffalo, NY: Christian Literature Publishing Co., 1894), 19.

33   Wilken, 48.

34   Irenaeus of Lyons, *Against the Heresies*, in Cyril Richardson, *Early Church Fathers* (New York: Collier, 1970), III.2.

35   Ibid., III.5.

36   Cited in Congregation for Catholic Education, *Instruction on the Study of the Fathers of the Church in the Formation of Priests* (Washington, D.C.: USCCB Publishing, 1989), footnote 14.

37   Cyril of Jerusalem, *On the Mysteries III*. trans. Edwin Hamilton Gifford, NPNF, Second Series, Vol. 7 (Buffalo: Christian Literature Publishing Co., 1894.), 1.

38   Gregory Nazianzen, *Letter 101: To Cledonius*, NPNF, Second Series, Vol. 7, 6.

39   A statement from the *Instruction on the Study of the Fathers of the Church in the Formation of Priests* is apt here: "As 'theologians,' they did not make use of the resources of reason only, but more properly, also of the religious resources gained through their affective existential knowledge, anchored in intimate union with Christ, nourished by prayer and sustained by grace and the gifts of the Holy Spirit. In their attitudes as theologians and pastors, they showed to a marked degree their deep sense of mystery and their experience of the divine that protected them from the ever recurring temptations both of exaggerated rationalism, or of a flat and resigned fideism" (37).

40   Athanasius of Alexandria, NPNF, Second Series, Vol. 4, 54.3.

41   Wilken, 25.

42   Augustine, *Confessions*, I.1.

43   Wilken, xviii.

44   Gregory of Nyssa, *To Eustathius: On the Holy Spirit*, trans. William Moore and Henry Austin Wilson, NPNF, Second Series, Vol. 5, 6.

45   Wilken, xviii.

46   Congregation for Catholic Education, *Instruction on the Study of the Fathers of the Church in the Formation of Priests*, 27.

47   Justin Martyr, "First Apology," in Cyril Richardson, *Early Church Fathers* (New York: Collier, 1970), 5.

48   Ignatius of Antioch, "Letter to the Philadelphians," in Cyril Richardson, *Early Church Fathers* (New York: Collier Books, 1970), 8.

49   Wilken, 15.

50   Ibid.

51   Ibid., 23.

52   Hilary of Poitiers, *On the Trinity*, trans. E.W. Watson and L. Pullan, NPNF, Second Series, Vol. 9, IX.3.

53   *Instruction*, 38.

54   Irenaeus of Lyons, *Against the Heresies*, in Cyril Richardson, *Early Church Fathers* (New York: Collier, 1970), I.10.

55   Cyprian of Carthage, *On the Unity of the Church*, trans. Robert Ernest Wallis, Ante-Nicene Fathers, Vol. 5, ed. Alexander Roberts, James Donaldson, and A. Cleveland Coxe (Buffalo, NY: Christian Literature Publishing Co., 1886), 6.

56   Clement of Rome, *First Letter to the Romans*, in *Early Christian Fathers*, edited by Cyril Richardson (New York: Collier Books, 1970), 14.

57   Willken, 46.

58   Clement of Rome, 7.

59   Wilken, 27.

60   Ibid. xx.

61   Ibid., 43.

62   Ibid.

63   *Instruction*, 28.

64   Augustine, *Against the Manicheans*, 5.6; cited in *Catechism of the Catholic Church*, #119.

65   Wilken, 25.

66   Ibid., 45.

67   Ibid., 42.

68   Ibid., 36.

69   Ignatius of Antioch, "Letter to the Ephesians," in Cyril Richardson, *Early Church Fathers* (New York: Collier, 1970), 13.

70   Cyril of Jerusalem, *On the Mysteries IV,* NPNF, Second Series, Vol. 7, 3 (with slight modifications).

71   Wilken, 49.

72   *Instruction*, 27.

73   Cyril of Jerusalem, *On the Mysteries V*, 22 (with slight modifications).

74   Augustine, *The Trinity*, XV.50.

75   Wilken, xvii.

76   Ibid., 6.

77   Ibid., 7.

78   Wilken, 174.

79   Ibid.

80   Wilken, 26.

81   Ibid., 311.

82   Ibid., 321.

Section 3

Models of Writing and Teaching

Balthasar's Approach to a Theology of God the Father

Theology at the Service of Spirituality

Margaret M. Turek, STD

Introductory Remarks

In his seminal essay, "Theology and Sanctity," Hans Urs von Balthasar spells out a program for the renewal of dogmatic theology.[1] At the center of this renewal is the re-integration of theology and spirituality. If theology and spirituality are allowed to interpenetrate and mutually determine each other, theological method will be enhanced and theological content, enriched. Furthermore, dogmatic theology, in undertaking this renewal, should extend its aims beyond the good of the discipline *per se*. Its renewal must be placed at the service of the renewal of the Church in holiness, whose renewal, in Her turn, is aimed at the renewal of the whole world in Christ. Theology is to enlighten, inspire, and shape Christian life, precisely so that Christian lives can offer a credible and effective witness to Christ in the world.

In fidelity to his own theological mission, Balthasar keeps these aims in view. He expounds on Christian revelation in a way that shows its vital connection with Christian life. He wants to show that the Christian mysteries provide patterns of relating and acting for the Christian life, and, conversely, that the Christian life testifies to (because it concretely embodies) the patterns of relating that derive from the Christian mysteries. To be sure, the pre-eminent and archetypal patterns of relating are derived from the mystery of the Trinity. Indeed, it belongs to the Trinitarian Father, as the unoriginated way of being God, to originally define the patterns of relating that proceed from Him (both *ad intra* and *ad extra*).

In what follows, I have gathered and interpreted Balthasar's scattered reflections on certain features of the Father's pattern of relating vis-à-vis the Son. I have framed the resultant sketch of the Father's way of being God within the context of the modern problem of a Father-God, a problem that largely stems from a flawed notion of the Father's almightiness. It is my hope that the theological method and content of this paper will not only offer an adequate response to this modern problem, but do so in a way that provides nourishment for devotion and illumination for the path to holiness, as Balthasar would have it. I will conclude with some comments on the implications of this theology of God's Fatherhood for the spirituality of the priest as "the parish spiritual father."[2]

The Modern Problem of a Father-God

From the confession of Jesus Christ as Son of God, there emerges a new understanding of God as Father, sovereign as the primal giver and model of freedom, in whom absolute power and authority coincide with perfectly selfless, other-directed love. This is a divine Fatherhood that has as the first purpose of its creative action to beget ("deify") human beings as beloved of God in the only Son. This is a way of being divine that glories in fathering "the glorious freedom of the children of God" (Rom 8:21).

The Christian confession of faith in precisely such an almighty God and Father has become increasingly obscured, however, by conflicting ideological, sociological, and philosophical perspectives. It stands in sharp contrast to that way of thinking which is dominant in our age, which associates the concepts of authority and power with those of domination and oppression. The protests raised by the modern criticism of religion and by atheistic humanism against the idea of an omnipotent Father-God appear to have lost little of their persuasive force. The contention that belief in a Father-God is antithetical to the dignity of the human person, that is, to his self-determination, reverberates in many domains of modern thought and culture.

The factors that have contributed to this concept are many and diverse. From the vantage point of social psychology, Alexander Mitscherlich regards as intolerable the Christian belief that human beings are called to be children of God. In his work, *Society Without the Father*,[3] he alleges that the idea of an all-powerful heavenly Father functions by controlling others; indeed a sanctioning of dictatorship is its inevitable outcome.[4] He interprets the relationship between a Father-God and human beings exclusively and entirely in terms of an omnipotence-impotence relationship. Humanity, he claims, has projected onto the screen of the heavens a divine counterpart to the feeling of impotence that characterizes the experience of little children.[5] Since, to his mind, belief in a personal omnipotent God can be perpetuated only so long as humanity associates the religious sense with the sense of impotence, it is understandable why Mitscherlich insists that the ongoing maturation of humanity requires an abandonment of the idea of God as almighty Father and a deliberate advancement towards a society "sufficiently adult to be able to leave him in order to stand on its own feet."[6] In his view, human society without an almighty Father-God means emancipation for humanity.[7]

That Mitscherlich interprets the relationship between a personal God and human beings solely in terms of an omnipotence-impotence relationship is not entirely accounted for on the basis of his social-psychological theory of the absolutization of the parent-child relationship. Evidently, the notion of God that Mitscherlich considers as representative of "religion," and specifically of Christianity, is that of Martin Luther.[8] In Luther's view, God's omnipotence rules out the possibility that God could allow His almighty will to be "dependent" on anything else—certainly not on a creature's freedom of will vis-à-vis Himself.[9] Like Augustine, Luther holds that no one can resist God's will.[10] But unlike Augustine, Luther *denies* human freedom a *cooperative* role in its encounter with divine freedom. Human freedom is not unfailingly persuaded to actively cooperate (which is Augustine's view), but remains *purely passive* in relation to the overpowering force of the divine will. For Luther, the proper counterpart of omnipotence can only be impotence.

Others have shown that the modern criticism of religion and systematic atheism arose largely in reaction to this defective doctrine of an all-powerful deity.[11] If, indeed, infinite freedom and finite freedom are mutually exclusive, the solution proposed by Ludwig Feuerbach is justifiable: in order that the dignity of human beings as self-determining persons be restored and secured, it is necessary that humanity be "saved," not *by* this God, but *from* this God.[12]

Plainly, Christianity today is facing a unique "apologetic" challenge, namely, to restore the mystery of the almighty God and Father of Jesus Christ to its central place in theological discourse. This restoration cannot be done without renovating the notion of divine omnipotence on the way to resolving the problem of how there can be a real interplay between infinite and finite freedom.

The God and Father of Jesus Christ

"Whoever has seen me has seen the Father.... [T]he Father who dwells in me is doing his works ... believe because of the works themselves" (Jn 14:9-11).[13] Balthasar discerns a twofoldness in the *dramatis persona* of Jesus. Jesus is at once the expression of the Father *and* his own active imitation of the way His Father is God. While Jesus knows that the Father works in Him, He is equally aware that what is required of Him is a total self-investment in the tasks He is sent to carry out. This twofold structure of Jesus' *persona* can be sufficiently explained, says Balthasar, if we grant that the Father gives over to the incarnate Son an "area" for collaborative activity, in which "area" the Son is left free, vis-à-vis the Father's work.[14] Metaphorically speaking, just as the playwright leaves room in his work for the actor to interpret the role, so the Father leaves Jesus the "space" for a personal exercise of freedom to accomplish the mission. The Son-Actor is not a "slave" of the Father-Author's "text."[15] Rather, "he knows that he has identified himself *in complete inner freedom* with the task that has been given to him."[16] In brief: the Father simultaneously "makes space" for the Son's exercise of human freedom and makes request of Jesus to freely "*allow* the Father to perform his fatherly works in him."[17]

Casting light on the freedom of the One Sent—the freedom to permit the Father to work in Him—enables Balthasar to perceive *the dramatic quality of the Father's involvement* in the mission of Jesus. For the Father's work that Jesus is summoned to let be accomplished is the work of begetting the Son *as man* to be His definitive image and revealer. Throughout the course of His earthly existence, Jesus is summoned to let the Father produce in His humanity the perfect, unparalleled likeness to the Father (cf. Jn 1:18; 5:19-20; 14:9-11; 15:9). This aim lies at the heart of Jesus' obedience. Now, if the Father coincides with His personal action,[18] then in calling Jesus to willingly collaborate with His paternal work, the Father *delivers Himself over* to Jesus' free decision. And conversely, if Jesus, on *His* side, realizes His freedom by reciprocally "making space" for the Father's work in Him (thus in filial fashion entrusting *Himself* to another), this "making space" can be seen as His active imitation of the Father's form of freedom. Indeed, if Jesus learns obedience through what He suffers (cf. Heb 5:8), His obedience is elicited by reason of His seeing in His Father a love which, in bestowing freedom, is willing to "suffer" the beloved's exercise of freedom without revoking the gift.[19]

Consequently, Balthasar discerns a *self-determined dependency* on the part of the Father vis-à-vis His Son, Jesus. The Father does not speak, act, or give Himself to be known apart from the Son (cf. Lk 10:27). Inasmuch as the Father leaves Jesus free, the Father lets Himself be dependent on the Son's free imitative response through which alone the Father's self-expression can be fulfilled "economically" (in terms of Jesus' humanity). But lest we misconstrue the Father's way of being dependent, we need to appreciate its evocative efficacy—its power to call forth the imaging response of filial freedom. We must avoid conceiving the Father's self-initiated dependency to be such that He holds Himself at a purely passive and impotent distance over and against Jesus' freedom. What needs to be grasped is that the Father's way of letting Himself be dependent is a modality of His generative love and for this reason is integral to the inwardly active and efficacious influence of the Father on the freedom of the Son.

Following on these considerations, Balthasar invites us to perceive that in the Father's pattern of relating, there is a unity of omnipotence and "weakness"—an *"all-powerful powerlessness..* The way in which the Father addresses the freedom of Jesus suggests a paternal love sufficiently all-powerful to show due regard for the autonomy of the beloved, and even to present itself as "defenseless" before the beloved's decision. Indeed, the almighty Father allows Himself to be "defenseless" precisely because He loves perfectly. For perfect love entails a selflessness that it is willing to expose itself to the one loved. And love which is "almighty" is powerful enough to be able to hand itself over to be accepted or rejected, without giving thought to protecting itself. Of singular import, for Balthasar, is that such recklessness and defenselessness—in virtue of its signaling the astonishing sublimity of the Father's love—has the power to evoke from the beloved the answer of love which it seeks. Indeed, God the Father's "defenselessness" proves omnipotent, since in delivering Himself over to the disposal of the One Sent, the Father engenders in Jesus an entirely grateful, "Yes," to His paternal self-donation, which Jesus reiterates throughout His mission. When, therefore, Jesus displays docility in handing Himself over to another (to the Sanhedrin, to Pilate), His pattern of acting is His concrete exegesis of the "all-powerful powerlessness" inherent in the Father's archetypal form of freedom.

In order to render more intelligible the *generative efficacy* of the Father's form of infinite freedom, Balthasar has recourse to a Scripturally inspired inter-subjective ontology, such as is represented by the parent-child model, which he considers to be an "*imago Trinitatis.*"[20] Balthasar's analysis of the parent-child relationship focuses on the "original experience" in which a little child is awakened to his being a person thanks to the call of love conveyed in his parent's smile. The parent's smiling and total giving of self, when beheld and understood as such by the little child, elicits a mirroring response. It is a response evoked and empowered in the face of the parent's self-donation. Love, devoted and dependable, is what enables the child to experience parental power and authority "as something other than a threat, since it is lived as a situation in which the parents' ever-latent love may be realized always anew."[21] The child adopts the dispositions of "docility ... trust and sweet surrender," dispositions that "are not for him virtues to be achieved but the most unreflectedly natural things in the world," because he has been the beneficiary of authority and power informed by love.[22] In short: within the context of an I-Thou relation of authentic interpersonal love, the child's capacity to give himself points back to the love he has first been shown.[23]

The application of an inter-subjective paradigm to the "economic" relationship of the Son with the Father underpins Balthasar's interpretation of John 5:19-20. "Amen, amen, I say to you, a son cannot do anything on his own, but only what he sees his father doing; for what he does, his son will do also. For the Father loves his Son and shows him everything that he himself does." The infinite freedom of the Father is not "shown" the Son other than in its self-determined form as a paternal self-giving-over or self-abandonment. It is precisely this, the Father's form of infinite freedom, that the incarnate Son deems as "the object of infinite amazement, wonderment and gratitude," worthy of unreserved reciprocation in the form of filial imitation.[24] For its part, Jesus' amazement "derives from a much deeper amazement of the eternal Child who, in the absolute Spirit of Love, marvels at [the archetypal mode of] Love itself."[25] Freedom, as primally defined by the Father's self-disposing, presents itself to the Son as a personal appeal so sublimely appealing in its form that it incites in Him a total assenting correspondence. As for the autonomy (divine and human) that the Son receives, it is always already given as the power to answer love with love; it is an autonomy proceeding from the paternal font of freedom in the form-quality of surrender of self to the other.

The Inner-Divine Fatherhood of God

Still to be addressed is the matter of extrapolating from the concrete, historical pattern of Jesus' relationship with the Father to the mystery of generation in God. Balthasar's sketch of the Fatherhood of God results in large measure from his applying in earnest the Trinitarian axiom that the historical mission of the Son is the (free) extension of His eternal procession from the Father.

Among the inferences which Balthasar makes is that the interplay of freedom between the Sender and the One Sent presupposes a relationship of reciprocal self-disposing between the Father and the Son in the eternal, immanent life of God.[26] Accordingly, the obedience of the incarnate Son, which traverses the entirety of His mission, is seen as a human expression of the Son's divine and eternal, "Yes," to the generating Father.[27] And with a shift of focus to the paternal Source, Balthasar proposes that if the Father's sending the Son is a temporal translation of His begetting the Son, then in the inner-divine Trinity, the Father "leaves-free the Begotten,"[28] allows the Son a distinct personal exercise of the divine will in relation to His act of generating.[29]

Once we grant that the Father-Begetter gives the Son "space" for an exercise of infinite freedom vis-à-vis Himself, we are positioned to take seriously Balthasar's correlative proposal that there is *in the Son* a "letting-be" [*Seinlassen*] or a "letting-happen" [*Geschehenlassen*] that corresponds to the Father's self-surrender, and "which is just as eternal as the act by which it is brought forth; indeed it is *implicit* [*mitgesetzt*] within this act."[30]

Consequently, if, as Balthasar asserts, "the realms of freedom in God come about both through the self-giving of the hypostases and by each hypostasis, *in turn*, letting the other two 'be,'"[31] we can interpret this insight according to the Trinitarian movement of divine love, and so locate in the Father the original disposition in which self-giving and letting-be coincide. Thus, the Father's self-giving includes, as intrinsic to it, a modality of letting-be that *begets in turn* its mirroring counterpart in the Son.[32]

Embedded in these reflections is the insight that, in the Father-Begetter, the ability to let-be the Begotten embraces both *omnipotence and powerlessness*. Earlier, we noted Balthasar's discernment of this paradox in regard to the Father's "economic" relationship with Jesus, and now, following Balthasar's style, we circle back round in order to throw light on its inner-divine root. If the Father, in begetting, leaves-free or lets-be the Son to answer paternal love with filial love, this freedom indicates a genuine "giving-over of power." For since the Father *is* His act of begetting, and if this act is eternally consummated only as coincident with the Son's begotten response of imaging love, then insofar as the Father allows the Son a distinct mode of divine freedom in relation to His act of generating, He, in effect, delivers over His Fatherhood to the Son's "seeing and deciding."[33] Yet, precisely this paternal "giving-over of power" is of infinite generative power.[34] "In the Father's act of generating," says Balthasar, "there lies, as it were, a request addressed to the Son, who on his side wishes nothing other than to meet the paternal will with his entire filial freedom."[35] The fact that the Son *"wishes nothing other than"* to assent to being begotten does not vitiate the eternal interplay of divine freedom, since this filial disposition is the infinitely free response of love engendered by love. The Father is all-powerful, since He can give without limit. At the same time, His is an omnipotent "powerlessness," since nothing is as truly powerful as the giving wherein He subjects His Paternity to the Son's "judgment." Indeed, the infinite power of paternal love's "powerlessness" is shown in the Son's limitless assent to being generated. But let there be no misunderstanding: it is not the Son's modality of letting-be that renders the Father's act omnipotent; to the contrary, it is the modality of letting-be proper to the Father that, as self-determined "weakness" in consideration of the beloved's freedom, engenders its answering reflection in the Son who lets Himself be begotten.

What all of this amounts to is a retrieval and recasting of the Trinitarian theology of the Greek Fathers. Like the Cappadocians, Balthasar is reticent to conceive the divine essence as ever existing in a "naked" state without circumscription by a personal manner of being God, and archetypally by the Father. Yet Balthasar advances beyond their use of sub-personal, naturalistic images of the Father's mode of divinity (e.g., the Father as torch or wellspring) to envision the patrogenetic dynamic of the trinitarian Godhead within the framework of a metaphysic of charity. This framework enables him to develop an understanding of the generative power of the Father's way of being divine that does not restrict itself to a notion of omnipotence fashioned principally by classical philosophy.[36] To be sure, Balthasar knows that it is possible to regard the efficacy of the Father's act of generating merely in respect to power as predicated of the divine (undifferentiated) substance: almightiness as conceived in treatises on the essential attributes of the Deity.[37] But to view the power of active generation in God solely from this vantage point cannot adequately perceive that it belongs to the Father to determine infinite power in the form-quality of triune self-surrender. For what constitutes the infinite power of God is identical with the tri-personal event of absolute, self-surrendering love that has its origin in the Father's way of being divine.[38] In Balthasar's words: the generating Father's almightiness

> can be none other than that of a surrender which is limited by nothing—what could surpass the power of bringing forth [the Son] 'equal in nature,' that is, equally loving

> and equally powerful, not another God but
> another in God? ... It is therefore essential,
> in the first instance, to see the unimaginable
> power of the Father in the force of his self-
> surrender, that is, of his love, and not, for
> example, in his being able to do this or that as
> he chooses.[39]

If this patrogenetic conception of the form-quality of the triune Godhead is taken into account when conceiving of the almightiness of the Father's generative act, the resultant understanding can maintain that if the Son, in eternal simultaneity, is uttered by the Father *and* answers to the Father with a Yes drawn forth vis-à-vis the Primal Lover, it is due to the efficacy of the Father's self-surrender (*how* He disposes of infinite freedom, His *manner* of exercising infinite power) to evoke the mirroring self-donation.

The Trinitarian Father and the Coexistence of Infinite and Finite Freedom

At this point, we begin our "descent" from the heights of the inner-divine Trinity to address the problem of the possibility of a real reciprocity between divine and human freedom.

The economy of Jesus Christ has revealed that the ultimate end of human existence consists in our being begotten of God the Father as adopted children in God the Son through the working of God the Holy Spirit (cf. Eph 1:3-

6; 1 Pt 1:3-5). Accordingly, the Father establishes us in an "acting area" of self-disposing, an "area" whose inner-divine ground is the infinite "acting area" of the Son.[40] Having been created and called in the *locus* of divine filial freedom, human freedom moves toward its self-realization by letting the Father beget in it an ever-greater likeness to Himself. Just as the eternal Son assents to being begotten in virtue of the efficacy of the Father's form of infinite freedom, and just as the incarnate Son willingly obeys in light of "seeing" all that the Father does (Jn 5:19-20), so human freedom's assent supposes an awareness of the inner disposition of the Primal Giver of freedom. To be persuasively moved to accept the call to be perfect as the heavenly Father is perfect (cf. Mt 5:48), "the creature must learn something of eternal love"; he must learn "how to 'see' God."[41] Thus the divine work of inducing human freedom to "hand itself over" includes, as an essential condition, a *revelatory* aspect. Commenting on the Son's commission from the Father, Balthasar notes that insofar as the Son's role is to "show" (Jn 14:8) or "make known" (Jn 1:18) the Father, it shares in the generative nature and aim of God's self-communication to human freedom. "Revelation," he says, with respect to the Son's mission, "means not only manifesting the Father's love in his own life ... but inviting and empowering [others] to imitate and reproduce it themselves."[42]

God's self-revelation does not nullify human freedom because infinite freedom, in disclosing itself, operates "in a latent manner which allows finite freedom to realize itself as genuine decision" for or against its being begotten of God.[43] The fact that human freedom is allowed to choose whether or not to let God "father" it by grace indicates that the self-revealing God "adopts a kind of incognito" in approaching finite freedom.[44] Such a choice requires that human freedom be situated among finite goods, which both point to and conceal God as the infinite, absolute good. Considered from God's side, "God's 'latency' is his loving respect for his creature's freedom;"[45] and this divine latency cannot be bypassed in any (temporal) encounter between infinite and finite freedom.

> The Father's Word, the Son, becomes 'flesh'... but the 'enlightening' brought about by this revelation...does not put an end to divine latency in favor of some kind of knowledge attainable without a decision on freedom's part. God is now [in Christ] more profoundly latent, and thus he makes both a greater gift of love to finite freedom and a greater challenge to it.[46]

I am led to still another consideration. If God's latency is linked with God's leaving free His creatures in relation to His generative love, we can regard the hiddenness of the self-revealing God as indicating God's willingness to engage with human freedom as one who renders himself "weak."

> God's all-powerful love is also 'powerlessness', not only giving the Son an equal, divine freedom but also giving the creature itself—the image of God—a genuine power of freedom and taking it utterly seriously.... [For] God does not overwhelm man; he leads him to his goals. This indicates no inability on

God's part.... It arises from the 'powerlessness' that, as we have seen, is identical with his omnipotence.[47]

The "powerlessness" of which Balthasar speaks concerns God's delivering over His Fatherhood (of grace) to the free creature's decision. While it is true that the divine offer permits the free creature to harden its heart against the Father's advances, nonetheless, the power to persuade the creature to "make space" for the Father's love arises, Balthasar maintains, from this very disposition of divine "powerlessness." Seeing that the Father is first to hand Himself over out of respect for our freedom, we, in our turn, are enabled to wager our lives on His will. The nonresistance that characterizes human freedom's surrender is a mirror image of the "defenseless" love tendered by the almighty Father.

Yet, to say that we are enabled to throw down our defenses is not to say that we are compelled to do so. The "weakness" of the almighty Father, as it is imaged in His Crucified Son, puts human freedom to the test. The test concerns our decision whether or not to stake our lives on the power of self-surrendering love as exemplified in the Crucified, or whether we will prefer to grasp at power in order to serve our interests and "make a name for ourselves" (Gen 11:4).

Implications for the Spiritual Fatherhood of the Priest

Space does not permit us to draw out of this theology a detailed consideration of the spiritual and pastoral implications relevant to the formation of priests. So I will limit myself to indicating some lines of reflection that merit further development.

Clearly, Balthasar's doctrine of God's Fatherhood precludes its abetting a notion of authority and power corrupted by the will to "lord it over" another and "make ... authority over [him] felt" (Mk 10:42). For while God the Father originally determines the form-quality of infinite freedom, this determination takes the form of an utterly selfless and generous love which wills to act for the good of others (cf. Mk 10:43-44). In this respect, Balthasar's notion of the Fatherhood of God portrays the archetype of every (derived) authority (cf. Eph 3:14-15) in a way which accords with the pertinent New Testament texts. Of particular significance is the analogy of proportionality which Paul sets up between the authority of God the Father vis-à-vis the Son, the authority of Jesus Christ vis-à-vis the Church, and the authority of the husband vis-à-vis the wife (1 Cor 11:3). In 1 Corinthians, Paul simply identifies the authoritative roles within the respective relations; in *Ephesians*, the proper exercise of authority is defined according to the example of Christ who "handed himself over" (Eph 5:25), so that His beloved "might be holy and without blemish" (v. 27; cf. 1:3-4). Johannine theology, in its turn, expands the horizon to illumine the power to call forth obedience that resides in the manner in which God—premierly as Father—exercises authority. In the *Gospel of John*, Jesus issues commands to His apostles as their master and teacher only after modeling for them the way He knows the Father to act as *His* head. "A Son...[can do] only what he sees his father doing; for what he does, his son will do also" (Jn 5:19); "As the Father loves me, so I also love you" (15:9); "If I ... have washed your feet, you ought to wash one another's feet. I have given you a model to follow, so that as I have done for you, you should also do" (Jn 13:14-15). For John, it is true in the first place of God the Father that authority in the form of self-forgetful foster-ance of the beloved (*auctoritas*, from *augere*: to make grow, to foster) is integral to inducing the response of obedience.[48]

Now as Jesus conferred upon his apostles the author-ity and power that He Himself received from the Father (cf. Mt 10:40; Lk 10:16; Jn 13:20; 17:18; 20:21), so the apostles, through the laying on of hands (cf. Acts 6:6; 1 Tim 4:14; 5:22; 2 Tim 1:6), called and empowered "other men as bish-ops, as priests and as deacons" to prolong the mission of Jesus and hence to "make present the very authority of God."[49]

Accordingly, if the priest is to represent divine au-thority, he must regularly contemplate Jesus's manner of exercising it and behold therein its eternal archetype: the Fatherhood of God. The priest ought to know the Father intimately as one who "sees" Him in the Son, so that he is spurred to dispose of his (derived) authority in like manner. Seeking God's "face" in prayer should be considered a pasto-ral priority, for the efficacy of the priest's spiritual paternity in some measure hinges on his imitation of the Father's pat-tern of relating toward His beloved. Pope John Paul affirms as much in *Pastores Dabo Vobis*:

> God's plan has ordained that the efficacy of
> the exercise of the ministry is also condi-
> tioned by ... the greater or lesser degree of the
> holiness of the minister.... This was clearly

stated by the Council: "The very holiness of priests is of the greatest benefit for the fruitful fulfillment of their ministry."[50]

Similarly, the Congregation for the Clergy argues that if Jesus Christ spoke and acted with authority,

> such authority derived, in the first place, from his divine condition but also, in the eyes of the people, from his sincere, holy and perfect example. Likewise, the priest is obliged to complement the objective spiritual authority which is his in virtue of sacred ordination with a subjective authority deriving from ... holiness of life, and that pastoral charity which manifests the love of Christ.[51]

Moreover, since the priest is to model divine authority according to the standard set by God the Father, then his contemplative beholding of God's Paternity (made visible in Christ's Sonship) should lead him to demonstrate an attitude of service toward the laity "to the point of a total gift of self."[52] Rather than imposing his weight on his parishioners, the priest is to rid himself of every trace of egotism and arrogance (cf. 1 Thes 2:5-8; 1 Pt 5:2-3). Indeed his pattern of relating to them should be sufficiently transparent to God's own, in order that his pastoral charity can be a stimulus of their free and loving response in the form of obedience.

Among the features of God's Fatherhood that the priest is called to mirror is the ability to "leave free" the laity, even as he unceasingly exhorts and encourages them to accept their share in Christ's mission. This "leaving free" requires that the priest be capable of enduring any amount of resistance to God's will which he encounters in his ministry, without revoking his pastoral charity. He must, with St. Paul, willingly suffer "labor until Christ be formed" in the faithful (Gal 4:19), without aborting his own mission. He is to exhibit gentleness, patience, and forbearance toward his parishioners, without downplaying the import of the gospel or minimizing its inherent demands (for the vocation to be begotten as sons and daughters in *the* Son is both a gift and a task). And through it all, the priest should be prepared to wager the efficacy of his spiritual paternity on the "weakness" of a self-handing-over which goes to the lengths of the Cross. Indeed, inasmuch as the priest delivers over the full expression of his fatherhood to the laity's free decision (since what he is to engender through his ministry is filial love and obedience to God), he must be made aware that he is called to take such a risk, to hazard such self-abandonment. To be sure, his concern should not be for himself, nor should he be riddled with anxiety in his pursuit of "successful results"; but he ought to leave the outcome of his self-giving in ministry with the heavenly Father, as Christ himself did.[53]

Final Remarks

In my estimation, Balthasar's theology of God the Father, by rescuing and purifying the conception of divine authority from distortions that envision it as tyrannical and despotic, can disarm those who would defend humanity against belief in a Father-God. Far from posing a threat to the dignity of human persons, the almighty God and Father of Jesus Christ makes Himself known as the ultimate fostering source of finite freedom. Indeed, to those who, like Mitscherlich, contend that the notion of God as Father is nothing but a projection of the seeming omnipotence of human fathers onto the screen of the heavens, Balthasar points out that the Fatherhood of God is the norm and the critical standard by which every creaturely exercise of authority and power is judged.

Furthermore, Balthasar's way of theologizing offers both seminary professors and seminarians an illustration of how to integrate doctrine and spirituality. Here is an approach to theology that places itself in the service of God's work of ongoing conversion and transformation in Christ. His theology begins with a contemplative beholding of the incarnate Word, and aims not only to heal the eyes of our hearts to "see" God, but also—and inseparably—to draw us to collaborate with God in the formation of saints ... and of saintly priests.

Notes

1   "Theology and Sanctity," in *Explorations in Theology: Vol. I, The Word Made Flesh* (Ignatius Press, 1989), 181-209.

2   James Keating, *Resting on the Heart of Christ: The Vocation and Spirituality of the Seminary Theologian* (Omaha: IPF Publications, 2009), 31.

3   Alexander Mitscherlich, *Society Without the Father: A Contribution to Social Psychology* (New York: Harcourt, Brace and World, Inc., 1963), 258.

4   See A. Mitscherlich, *op. cit.*, 37-39, and 251.

5   See A. Mitscherlich, *op. cit.*, 145.

6   A. Mitscherlich, *op. cit.*, 258.

7   In the Epilogue, Mitscherlich concurs with Karl Marx's definition of emancipation: "All emancipation is the reduction of the human world, of conditions, to man himself;" *op. cit.*, 305.

8   See A. Mitscherlich, *op. cit.*, 165, 176-177.

9   Paul Althaus sums up Luther's reasoning thus: "God determines everything with his almighty working, such that nothing and nobody can resist his will or restrict his activity. Because of his almighty activity, God has each man completely in his hand. God works everything in him. Luther, therefore, cannot even speak of man's freedom of will in relation to God and thus salvation [and perdition] are taken out of man's hand." P. Althaus, *The Theology of Martin Luther*, trans. by Robert C. Schultz (Philadelphia: Fortress Press), 110-111.

10   To be sure, the Church did not follow Augustine on this point.

11   See Karl Löwith, *From Hegel to Nietzsche* (New York: Anchor, 1967).

12   Henri de Lubac, in his analysis of Feuerbach's criticism of religion, sees it as based on "A Tragic Misunderstanding": The Christian God "began to seem [to modern man] like the enemy of his dignity....Humanity is getting rid of God in order to regain possession of the human greatness which, it seems to him, is being unwarrantably withheld by another. In rejecting God he is overthrowing an obstacle in order to gain his freedom." Henri de Lubac, *The Drama of Atheistic Humanism* (London: Sheed & Ward), 6.

13   See also Jn 4:34; 5:17,19,30; 6:57; 8:28-29; 10:37-38; 15:9-10; 17:4,7-8.

14   See *Theo-Drama III: Dramatis Personae: Persons in Christ* (San Francisco: Ignatius Press, 1992), 198, 532-34. Henceforth, *TD* 3. Also *Unless You Become Like This Child* (San Francisco: Ignatius Press, 1991), 64-5. Henceforth, *UYB*.

15   See *TD* 3, 532.

16   *TD* 3, 183. Emphasis mine.

17   *TD* 3, 519. Emphasis mine. Also, *You Have the Words of Eternal Life* (San Francisco: Ignatius Press, 1991), 154: "[W]hat Jesus does is permit the Father to work in him."

18   Just as, in the eternal and immanent life of the Trinity, God the Father *is* his generative act vis-à-vis his begotten Son, so in the economy of revelation and salvation God the Father *is* his generative work vis-à-vis his incarnate Son. If the former action (*ad intra*) is constitutive of God in himself, the latter action (*ad extra*) is the free and definitive prolongation of God's Fatherhood 'for us' in the Christ-event.

19   For a discussion of "The Paternal Affectivity of the Immutable God," see M. Turek's *Towards a Theology of God the Father: Hans Urs Von Balthasar's Theodramatic Approach* (New York: Peter Lang, 2001) 167-188.

20   Balthasar's usage of the insights of modern interpersonalist philosophy are intended only to serve an articulation of Scriptural revelation. What cannot be overly stressed is that the primary reality is the I-Thou relation in God which surpasses our apprehension at every point. The human person and its I-Thou relations are but faint reflections of it.

21   *UYB*, 18-19.

22   *UYB*, 22.

23   See "Movement Toward God," 15-17. The principal ideas of this extensive essay can also be found condensed and summarized in Chapter 2 ("The Human Child") of *UYB*, 15-25.

24   *UYB*, 45: "[W]hen the Father hands over everything to the Son, this 'everything' includes the Father's freedom. And precisely this handing-over is the object of infinite amazement, wonderment and gratitude."

25   *UYB*, 46.

26   Inasmuch as we can affirm "a real identity" between the Son in his immanent generation from the Father and the Son in his economic mission from the Father, we can affirm, in turn, "a real identity" between the Father in his immanent action and in his economic action vis-à-vis the Son. See the International Theological Commission in its 1981 document "Theology, Christology, Anthropology," *The Documents of the International Theological Commission: 1969-1985* (San Francisco: Ignatius Press, 1989), 219.

27   This serves to explain why Balthasar, in speaking of the freedom of Jesus Christ, lays stress upon its *filial* mode rather than upon the distinction between Jesus' infinite divine freedom and his finite human freedom. For in the incarnation of the Son, finite human freedom is assumed by the hypostatic mode of self-disposing that *is* the Son in his inner-divine relation to the

generating Father. Hence, if the intimate relation of the One Sent to the paternal Origin takes the form of obedience, it means that "absolute obedience can become the economic form of the Son's absolute [immanent] response to the Father;" *TD* 3, 530.

28   *Theo-drama II: Dramatis Personae: Man in God* (San Francisco: Ignatius Press, 1990), 257. Henceforth, *TD* 2. See in addition *Theo-Drama V: The Last Act* (San Francisco: Ignatius Press, 1998), 93. Henceforth, *TD* 5.

29   To be sure, the divine Son exercises the one essential will of the Godhead, but he does so by way of the non-reversible order of his eternal procession, and hence in his distinct hypostatic mode vis-à-vis the generating Father.

30   *TD* 5, 86.

31   *TD* 2, 262.

32   Of course, all that Balthasar has to say about the Father's elicitation of the Son's assent to his being generated remains based upon a conception of eternal life that precludes its being described as a becoming (as a movement from potency to act, from poverty to wealth, from before to after). The divine processions "which give rise to the fellowship of Persons are not subject to temporal limitation but are eternally operative" *TD* 5, 77-78.

33   In *Theo-Drama IV: The Action* (San Francisco: Ignatius Press, 1994), 319, Balthasar speaks of "the triune freedom of God which, in its unity, leaves each hypostasis its mode of seeing and deciding." And on 326, he states: The Son's "eternal Yes to being-given-himself as consubstantially divine" is an entirely grateful "Yes to the primal kenosis of the Father in the unity of omnipotence and powerlessness." Henceforth, *TD* 4. See also *TD* 5, 485.

34   See *TD* 5, 66.

35   *TD* 5, 88. In *TD* 2, 257-58, Balthasar argues that "since each hypostasis in God possesses the same freedom and omnipotence, we can speak of there being reciprocal petition [*gegenseitiger Bitte*]."

36   According to the ITC's 1981 document "Theology, Christology, Anthropology," 214, in classical philosophy "substance in general was at the center of things, but here [inasmuch as 'the mystery of God and man is shown to the world as the mystery of love'] the center is a 'metaphysic of charity,' namely, the person, whose most perfect act is the act of charity."

37   Divine power conceived as limitless according to the actual, infinite perfection of the divine substance; divine power as utterly unimpeded by any other principle; divine power as capable of doing all things that are possible absolutely. See, for example, Thomas Aquinas, *Summa Theologica*, Pt. 1, Q. 25, arts. 2 and 3.

38   "God the Son and the Holy Spirit" eternally act as Persons equal in divinity with the Father, "but still with [a divine freedom] that is originally grounded in [and informed by] the fatherly Origin. ...[The Father's self-donation] is the origin of all freedom—not in the sense of doing as one chooses, but in that of superior self-possession of the love which surrenders itself. This freedom is bestowed upon the Son along with divinity." *Credo: Meditations on the Apostles' Creed* (New York: Crossroad, 1990), 31-32. Henceforth, *Credo.*

39   *Credo,* 31.

40   "If God's nature, theologically speaking, shows itself to be 'absolute love' by giving itself away and allowing others to be,...the same must apply to his 'making room' for his free creatures"; *TD* 2, 272-73. In addition, *TD* 2, 266: "[T]he 'nothing-out-of-which' the world came into being can only be sought in infinite freedom itself: that is, in the realms of creatable being opened up by divine omnipotence and, at a deeper level, by the trinitarian 'letting-be' [*Seinlassen*] of the hypostatic acts." See also *TD* 2, 259.

41   *TD* 2, 276.

42   *TD* 3, 518.

43   *TD* 2, 316. See also *TD* 5, 88.

44   See *TD* 2, 273.

45   *TD* 2, 276.

46   *TD* 2, 275-76. See my article "Dare We Hope 'That All Men Be Saved'?: On Balthasar's Trinitarian Grounds for Christian Hope" in *Logos: A Journal of Catholic Thought and Culture.* 1 (1997) NR. 3, 92-121, for a discussion of the divine latency operative in the event of the Cross which allows the free creature to refuse to accept the God of Jesus Christ.

47   *TD* 4, 330-1. Pope John Paul II agrees: "Faith affirms that God is omnipotent;" nonetheless, "aren't we being presented with a sort of 'divine impotence'...? Yes, in a certain sense one could say that *confronted with our human freedom, God decided to make himself 'impotent'....* Before this gift [of human freedom] he remains consistent and *places himself before the judgment of man."* See *Crossing the Threshold of Hope* (New York: Alfred A. Knopf, 1994), 64-65; emphasis is the author's.

48   In *UYB*, 22-23, when analyzing the parent-child model as an *imago trinitatis,* Balthasar maintains that "it is the expressly perceivable egotism of the giver ('you who are evil') that results in the gift's no longer being understood as the image of the giver: only then...[do] we see vanish...obedience as the immediate response to the 'fostering' source; only then does concrete 'fosterance' (*auctoritas,* from *augere*: 'to make grow', 'to foster') become abstract, legal 'authority.'"

49   See Pope John Paul II, *Pastores Dabo Vobis*, Apostolic Exhortation On the Formation of Priests in the Circumstances of the Present Day, promulgated on March 25, 1992, 14-15 and 24. Henceforth, *PDV*.

50   Pope John Paul II, *PDV*, 25; inner citation is from *Presbyterorum Ordinis*, 12.

51   The Congregation for the Clergy in *The Priest and the Third Christian Millennium: Teacher of the Word, Minister of the Sacraments, and Leader of the Community* (USCC, 1999), 10. See also Joseph Cardinal Ratzinger's "The Ministry and Life of Priests" in *Pilgrim Fellowship of Faith* (San Francisco: Ignatius Press, 2005), 171.

52   Pope John Paul II, *PDV*, 15.

53   See Joseph Cardinal Ratzinger's "On the Essence of the Priesthood" in *Called to Communion: Understanding the Church Today* (San Francisco: Ignatius Press, 1996), 129.

Contemplating Christ in the Classroom

John Gresham, PhD

The heart of Christian catechesis is the Person of Jesus Christ. The goal of catechesis is to bring students into intimacy with Jesus Christ, that through Him, they might know the love of the Father through the gift of the Holy Spirit.[1] Moreover, in seminary formation, Christ provides the image and model for priesthood. An essential and permanent aspect of priesthood is the priest's call to "resemble Christ ... to live out Christ's spousal love toward the Church, His bride." The priest is called to "reveal to others, in Jesus Christ, the true face of God, and as a result the true face of humanity." To do this, the priest himself must seek the face of God and "contemplate it with loving veneration."[2] Therefore, when he spoke to seminarians at the 2005 World Youth Day in Cologne, Pope Benedict XVI emphasized that the "deepest goal" of seminary formation "is to bring the student to an intimate knowledge of the God who has revealed his face in Jesus Christ." The Pope exhorted every seminarian gathered in Cologne to learn from Mary to "contemplate Jesus with the eyes of the heart and to make Jesus his very life."[3]

At some level, every course in the seminary curriculum has Christ as its subject and goal. Pope Benedict XVI reminds us that "even when, as in Canon Law and in Church History, the immediate object is the People of God in its visible, historical dimension, the deeper analysis of the topic urges us once again to contemplation, in the faith, of the mystery of Risen Christ."[4] Yet, if Christ is at the center of all theological formation, then the course in Christology has particular importance. The course in Christology is a privileged moment in which intellectual formation has as its exact subject matter that which is at the very heart of all seminary formation. Thus, the Christology course provides a strategic opportunity for the integration of intellectual and spiritual formation. This essay focuses on the Christology course as a model for such integration in the hopes that its suggestions will stimulate similar reflections on other courses across the curriculum. We must begin by asking the following questions: If the Christology course truly touches the heart of formation, is this course all it can be? Do we teach this course in such a way that our students merely come to know a lot about Christ without, at the same time, growing to know Christ in a deeper way? In addition to gaining a lot of information about Christ, does our course help the seminarians gain greater intimacy with Christ? Can they grow to resemble Christ in a deeper way as a result of this course in Christology? Of course, we pray and trust in God's grace to initiate and sustain this growth; but is there more we might do to cooperate with Christ's own desire for union with these seminarians? Are there ways to transform how we teach Christology in order to better facilitate our seminarians' growth in communion with Christ?

What is needed is a contemplative approach to teaching and studying Christology that is shaped by the loving gaze upon the face of Christ as the face of God. An outline for such a contemplative approach is found in John Paul II's vision for the Church in the third millennium. In his apostolic letter *Novo Millennio Ineunte*, John Paul II emphasized that the program for the new millennium is what it has been throughout the history of the Church. This program "has its centre ... Christ himself, who is to be known, loved and imitated, so that in him we may live the life of the Trinity, and with him transform history until its fulfillment in the heavenly Jerusalem."[5] The Church's task is to reflect the light of Christ and to make the face of Christ shine before the generations of the new millennium. But in order to do so, we must first, ourselves, take time to contemplate the face of Christ.[6] Thus, the heart of this apostolic letter consists of John Paul II's extended reflection on contemplating the face of Christ. In what follows, we look to this reflection to provide a perspective for a contemplative approach to the mystery of Christ, containing hints on how we may teach Christology in such a way as to foster intimacy with Christ and transformation into the image of Christ. We will add to John Paul II's suggestions certain parallels to be found in Pope Benedict XVI's essay "Taking Bearings in Christology" in which he wrote as Cardinal Ratzinger on "a theological basis for a spiritual Christology."[7] Along the way, we will also note recent works in New Testament Christology and related disciplines that may offer confirmation and further support for these reflections.

A Contemplative Quest for the Historical Jesus

John Paul II emphasizes that the gospels provide a vision of faith "based on precise historical testimony." Neither the complexity of the gospels' literary redaction nor their primary kerygmatic catechetical purpose detracts from their trustworthy and true testimony. From the gospels, *"the face of the Nazarene emerges with a solid historical foundation."*[8] John Paul II reiterates the teaching of *Dei Verbum* and the Catechism of the Catholic Church that the gospels give us the "honest truth about Jesus."[9] The contention that the traditions behind the gospels are rooted in eyewitness testimony finds recent scholarly support in Richard Bauckham's study of gospel origins.[10] But John Paul II goes on to emphasize that historical study alone does not enable us to see the face of Christ. Not only those separated from Him by historical distance as we are, but even Jesus's own contemporaries did not recognize who He was apart from faith in the mystery of His Person. John Paul II recalls the skepticism of Thomas the Apostle and claims that even touching and seeing the risen Lord is not enough apart from faith: "regardless of how much his body was seen or touched, only faith could fully enter the mystery of that face."[11] John Paul II reminds us of the twelve apostles' own confusion when Jesus asked them, first "Who do people say that I am?" (Mk 8:27) And then, more personally and directly, "But who do you say that I am?" (Mk 8:29) The grace of divine revelation enables Peter to confess Jesus' true identity. "Only the faith proclaimed by Peter, and with him by the Church in every age, truly goes to the heart, and touches the depth of the mystery."[12] From the experience of these first witnesses, John Paul concludes the necessity of grace and the essential role of prayer for coming to know Jesus: "We cannot come to the fullness of contemplation of the Lord's face by our own efforts alone, but by allowing grace to take us by the hand. Only the experience of silence and prayer offers the proper setting for the growth and development of a true, faithful, and consistent knowledge of that mystery."[13] As we begin to study the history of Jesus revealed through the gospels, we, too, in the seminary classroom, must approach that study with a great awareness of our need for grace and with the spirit of prayer and silence by which we prepare ourselves for that grace.

The essential role of prayer in the quest for the historical Jesus was also emphasized by Pope Benedict. A study of the gospels leads to the discovery of Jesus' prayer to the Father as revealing the very heart and meaning of His identity. Jesus' whole life is lived as a prayer, and even His death is transformed into a prayerful offering of Himself to His Father. To enter into a historical understanding of this life in its mysterious depths, Pope Benedict argues, it is necessary to enter into the prayer of Jesus. This prayer is not just some "pious supplement to reading the Gospels" but rather, "it is the basic precondition of real understanding." Thus, "all real progress in theological understanding has its origin in the eye of love and in its faculty of beholding."[14] While this prayer is very personal and touches each individual, it is not individualistic, for this prayer presupposes the community founded by Jesus as the place of prayer. Pope Benedict concluded this study with the words, "Christology is born of prayer or not at all."[15]

If prayer is so central to Christological understanding, should it not be more central to our study of Christology in the seminary classroom? Some of the most challenging passages in James Keating's call to integrative seminary teaching are when he speaks of prayer and silence in the classroom.[16] We are very jealous of our classroom time, filling each and every minute with as much information as we can squeeze into the course. We must not be afraid to include time for prayer if we want our students to know Christ. In order to welcome such time, we must first of all resist the pressure to fill our classes, as well as our preparation prior to class, with frenetic activity. With all the demands placed on both seminarians and faculty, it is easy to fall prey to a rushed and busy pace that carries over into a hurried presentation in the classroom that imparts lots of information but allows little opportunity for silence and reflection. We need to replace the feverish busyness with a backdrop of silence. [17] Within that silence, we study and prepare for class; and out of that silence, we speak of the mysteries of the faith to our seminarians. At times, we may pause in class and invite them to enter that silence and to gaze with us upon the mystery of Christ. To assist us in slowing the pace of the classroom, we might periodically project an appropriate quote, relevant to the day's topic, and pause and invite a moment of silent reflection. Instead of speeding through our PowerPoint presentations, we might create such pauses in our presentation that allow for moments of prayer and silence.

If we want our students to study their assigned texts from a backdrop of prayer and silence, we may need to rethink the amount of reading we assign. Our concern for the essential information that the students must cover in the course might be better met by fewer pages read deeply and reflectively than by more pages read rapidly and sometimes superficially. Through careful selection of primary and secondary sources, we may accomplish more with less. To simply cover information, assigned articles from reference works can be used to provide concise but thorough overviews. Assigning only selected portions of a text book might just whet our students' appetites to read further, even after the course is completed. With more judicious choices in assigned readings, we may find room in our syllabus to include some spiritual reading as an aide to the student's prayerful interaction with these concepts.[18]

We can also incorporate assignments that require prayer and bring the fruit of prayer into the classroom. One enriching exercise that I have used is to have each student select a different title from the *Litany of the Holy Name of Jesus* or the *Litany of the Sacred Heart of Jesus*. They are to study the biblical and historical background and linguistic meanings behind their selected title; but just as importantly, they are to make the title a personal prayer to Jesus. Then, each class begins with a different student offering a brief meditation on their title for Jesus in which they share the fruit of their

prayer with classmates. The students conclude their meditation by leading us all in a prayer to Jesus under that particular
title. Thus, by participation in this prayer of the Church, this
litany leads us to a deeper understanding of Christ born out
of prayer. One could do a similar assignment with the titles
of Christ in Scripture, integrating historical-critical study of
Christological titles with prayerful meditation. This actually
puts the student in touch with the historical origins of these
titles in early Christian faith and worship.[19] So, for example,
from the early Christian Aramaic prayer, "Maranatha" to the
Christ hymn in the second chapter of Philippians, the Christological title "Lord" emerged historically in an experience
of profound worship of Christ. To join in that worship today
does not undermine a historical-critical study of the title but
rather, enables the seminarian to share in that experience of
the Spirit which first enabled those early Christians to pray,
"Jesus is Lord!"

Gazing on the Face of Christ in Scripture

In *Novo Millennio Ineunte*, John Paul II reminds us
again of St. Jerome's famous phrase, "Ignorance of Scripture
is ignorance of Christ," and the Pope calls us to a canonical
approach which contemplates Christ's face prefigured in the
Old Testament and revealed fully in the New.[20] While his reflection on the face of Christ in this apostolic letter is rooted
in Scripture, John Paul does not offer much in the way of ex-
plicit exegetical guidance for teaching biblical Christology.
Yet, there are a couple of insights to be found in his reflection

that could assist us in adding a contemplative dimension to our study and teaching of biblical Christology.

First, John Paul reminds us that we read Scripture in order to discover and gaze upon the face of Christ. It is quite easy in biblical studies to have our gaze deflected away from Christ. We may focus on the theological interests of the final redactor of a biblical text, the ecclesial issues within the community for which the text was composed, the social and cultural context reflected by the text, and so on. All are important aspects of scriptural interpretation, but we can never forget that we look "through" these aspects as part of the lens which enables us to focus on that which the texts themselves focus: the mystery of Jesus Christ. I find Richard Burridge's studies of gospel genre quite helpful in this regard. While his studies are obviously not biographies in the modern sense, he has made a strong and widely accepted case that the gospels are, in fact, very much in the genre of Greco-Roman biography. Burridge criticizes biblical scholars for reading the gospels as if they were "by committees, for communities, about theological ideas." Based on the genre of the gospels, he argues that their primary subject matter is a person.[21] The significance of this rediscovery of the biographical intent of the gospels is to remind us of the obvious but all too often forgotten point that the gospels are in fact about Jesus! We do not read them primarily to speculate about a community by which and for which they were supposedly composed but as a means to know and contemplate the face of Jesus.

A second insight from *Novo Millennio Ineunte* that might provide a fruitful way of contemplating the face of Christ in Scripture is found in John Paul's reference to the

Church's living memory of Jesus. Citing St. Bernard's hymn "Jesu dulcis memoria," John Paul II describes the Church as remembering the events from Jesus's life as if they happened today. Because She remembers one who is risen and lives, the Church's memory leads Her to gaze as a bride on the face of Christ in Scripture, the face of Her treasure and joy.[22] Mary, who contemplated the mystery of Jesus in her heart, provides the model for our imitation.[23] John Paul II sees Mary as a symbol and icon of the maternal memory of the Church. In her tradition, the Church bears, treasures, and transmits the memory of Jesus.[24] Pope Benedict, too, emphasizes that we come to know Jesus in communion with the Church, who bears the memory of Jesus in Her tradition, a memory in which the past becomes present through the presence of Jesus alive in the Church.[25] There is a Marian contemplative dimension to Scripture study which reads the bible as a living repository of the Church's memory of Jesus by which we come to know our Lord as a living presence. Recent studies in New Testament Christology suggest that memory is a helpful category for interpreting the biblical witness to Jesus.[26] The communal dimension of the Church's memory is reflected in Philip Esler's approach to New Testament theology. Within the living communion of saints, the New Testament authors still speak to us and share with us their memory of Jesus and witness to Him. Reading and studying Scripture is like a form of interpersonal and intercultural communication with our brothers and sisters in Christ from another time and culture.[27] These approaches suggest a way of synthesizing careful historical-critical study with a contemplative reading of Scripture. Careful historical and linguistic study assists us to understand these past witnesses to Jesus. Through our communion with them in the Church, we share in their memory of Jesus and with them gaze upon our living Lord.

Contemplating Christ with the Fathers of the Church

In *Novo Millennio Ineunte*, John Paul II's comments on Chalcedon suggest how we might add a contemplative dimension to our study and teaching of the Christological councils. He says the Chalcedonian formula, despite the intrinsic limitations of all human concepts and words, "enables us ... to gaze in some way into the depths of the mystery ... Jesus is true God and true man." John Paul II compares the Church to the apostle Thomas, invited by Christ to touch his wounds, to recognize the "fullness of his humanity ... clothed in the fullness of his divine splendor," exclaiming in adoration, "My Lord and My God."[28] Thus, John Paul reminds us of the doxological dimension of the Christological formulations. Pope Benedict has also emphasized how the Christological formulas are rooted in prayer. He describes the Nicene "homoousion" as the philosophical translation of Jesus' experience of prayer to the Father. By this language, the Church affirms that Jesus' union with the Father revealed by His living prayer is no mere metaphor but an ontological reality.[29]

As with our study of Scripture, as we begin to study and teach these councils, it is easy to divert our gaze from their primary object, the mystery of Jesus Christ. Reading the councils from the perspective of enculturation, we focus on the cultural and philosophical categories employed by the Fathers. We may focus on the ecclesiastical conflicts and rhetorical strategies surrounding each council, or we may focus on the patristic patterns of reading Scripture reflected in the Christological debates. All of these are significant aspects for interpreting the teachings of the Fathers and the early Church Councils. And yet, they may deflect our gaze from Jesus Himself. Can we look with the councils at the mystery of Jesus Christ, God-made-man? Can our study of the councils lead to adoration of Christ as described by John Paul II? In a recent essay, patristic scholar John McGuckin has also urged us to recover the doxological origins of the Christological formulations. He reminds us that the Council Fathers took their formulations from existing baptismal and other liturgical formulations. The Christological formulas originate in worship. In his essay, McGuckin recasts the wording of Chalcedon, transposing its phrases from the language of anathema to the language of praise, in order to highlight its original doxological character.[30] This transpositioning suggests a technique that we might use in our classes. Either the instructor or the students might compose similar transpositions of each council (not only the ecumenical councils but other important Christological formulations such as the Eleventh Council of Toledo). Thus, for example, part of the Chalcedonian definition transposed as prayer might read: *Lord Jesus Christ, you are perfect in deity, perfect in humanity. You are truly God and truly Man. You are one in being with*

*the Father as to your divinity and you are one in being with us
as to your humanity, like us in all things but sin...*

These rephrased texts could be prayed in class, or
the students could be encouraged to use them in their own
prayer before the Blessed Sacrament. Through such prayer,
the seminarians, rather than simply trying to master these
Christological teachings, would use these formulations to
enter more deeply into adoration of the mystery of Jesus.

John Paul II also emphasizes the anthropological
and soteriological dimension of the Christological teaching
of the councils. In the incarnation, Jesus reveals the face of
God; but at the same time, because He is both God and Man,
Jesus "reveals to us also the true face of man, "fully revealing
man to man himself."[31] Thus, in this exhortation at the dawn
of the new millennium, John Paul, as he did at the dawn of
his pontificate, recalls once again the teaching of Vatican II
that "only in the mystery of the Incarnate Word does the
mystery of man take on light"[32] In the face of Jesus, we contemplate the new divinized humanity in which we are called
to share. Pope Benedict also emphasized this soteriological
dimension of the Christological councils, emphasizing in
particular the contribution of the sixth ecumenical council
and the teaching of Maximus the Confessor. The authentic
freedom of Jesus' human will in union with His filial will as
the divine Son points the way to our freedom through obedience.[33] Christ reveals and makes possible a new humanity
which finds freedom through humble service. This vision
of human life comes as a "shock" that demands continuous
conversion.[34] This call to be configured to Christ in His humility, obedience, and service is addressed to all Christians,

but has particular and specific reference to those who are forming their lives to serve the faithful as an "alter Christus." In teaching the Christology of the Ecumenical Councils, we must draw our students' attention to their soteriological and anthropological dimension and highlight its relevance to the priestly vocation.

Just as Pope Benedict enjoins us to follow the further Christological development beyond Chalcedon in the sixth ecumenical council, I think it is important to lead seminarians in the Christology course to the seventh ecumenical council on the veneration of images of Christ. Christ imaged in the icon upholds orthodox faith in the reality of the incarnation and refutes all the heresies condemned in previous ecumenical councils.[35] The *Catechism of the Catholic Church* reflects that same perspective when it moves from the Christological councils on to the seventh ecumenical council and, from there, on to the later devotion to the Sacred Heart.[36] In these sacred images, we see the mystery of Christ concretely symbolized for our veneration. Such sacred images of Jesus should be brought into the classroom to help us move from a merely discursive understanding of the Christological formulas to a more contemplative gaze upon the face and heart of Christ. These images provide a point of integration between an intellectual study of the Christological mystery defined in Church Councils and the interior grasp of those mysteries in the devotional life of the faithful.

Contemplating the Face of Christ Crucified and Risen

John Paul II describes the cross as the "the most paradoxical aspect of his [Christ's] mystery ... The mystery within the mystery, before which we cannot but prostrate ourselves in adoration ... We shall never exhaust the depths of this mystery."[37] He describes Jesus' passion as both profound agony and profound unity with the Father. "At the very moment when he identifies with our sin, 'abandoned' by the Father, he 'abandons' himself into the hands of the Father." To grapple with this great mystery, John Paul II turns to the wisdom to be found in the "lived theology" of the saints. Citing examples from St. Catherine of Siena and of St. Therese of Lisieux, he finds in the dark night of these saints a personal experience "akin to Jesus's experience on the Cross in the paradoxical blending of bliss and pain."[38] This suggests that as we grapple with the mystery of the cross in our seminary classroom, perhaps we, too, must turn to the saints as well. Their experience of bliss and pain reminds us that the mystery of the cross is something in which we share. In their accounts of the relation between the cross of Jesus and our sharing in that cross, the saints highlight a biblical theme: cruciformity. New Testament scholar Michael Gorman has shown the centrality of this "cruciformity" in St. Paul's Christology and soteriology. He describes St. Paul's soteriology as a kenotic cruciform theosis through Spirit-enabled co-crucifixion with Christ.[39] Our teaching on the cross of Christ must integrate Christology with a spirituality of the cross as reflected in Scripture and illuminated by the

writings of the saints. I suspect that many of the difficulties
that we encounter in understanding the cross are due to interpreting theologies of atonement as philosophical theories
abstracted from the spirituality of the cross which informs
them. To give just one example, I have found St. Anselm's
Cur Deus Homo illumined when read in light of the spirituality reflected in his *Prayers and Meditations*.[40] Especially
when teaching those discerning a call to image the kenotic
cruciform Christ as His priests, we must integrate our theology of the cross with the lived spirituality of the cross.

John Paul II concludes his contemplation of the face
of Christ in chapter II of *Novo Millennio Ineunte* by considering the face of Jesus risen from the dead. John Paul cites I
Corinthians 15:17, "If Christ has not been raised, [our] faith
is vain" and recalls the life-changing encounters with the
risen Lord experienced by St. Peter and St. Paul. The Church
today, from Her encounter with the risen Lord, derives the
strength to proclaim Christ in the new millennium.[41] John
Paul II's reflection suggests the importance of the present
encounter with the risen Lord. We may enter into a dialogue
with the Lord today. Such dialogue with the risen Lord is an
essential aspect of the priestly vocation. "The history of every priestly vocation, as indeed of every Christian vocation,
is the history of an inexpressible dialogue between God and
human beings, between the love of God who calls and the
freedom of individuals who respond lovingly to Him."[42] To
foster such dialogue in the Christology course, we might
take as a model the chapter on "Jesus the Abiding Presence"
in Gerald O'Collins's recent literary portrait of Jesus.[43]
O'Collins presents a series of questions asked by Jesus in the

fourth gospel and invites us to respond to them as questions that Jesus addresses to us today: "What are you looking for? Will you also go away? Do you believe this? Do you know what I have done to you? Have I been with you so long, and yet you do not know me? Why are you weeping? Who are you looking for? Do you love me?" Those of us responsible for teaching Christology to seminarians might create a reflective assignment in which each seminarian takes one of these questions and others from the gospels and enters into a dialogue in which he answers Jesus's questions; or, more importantly, perhaps we, as instructors, should spend time with Jesus to hear and answer His questions.

Notes

1   John Paul II, *Catechesi tradendae* (1979), 5.

2   John Paul II, *Pastores Dabo Vobis* (1992), 5, 22, 72.

3   Pope Benedict XVI, "Address to Seminarians", August 19, 2005 in *God's Revolution: World Youth Day and Other Cologne Talks* (San Francisco: Ignatius Press, 2006), 47-8.

4   Pope Benedict XVI, "Visit of the Holy Father to Pontifical Gregorian University," November 3, 2006 cited in James Keating, *Resting on the Heart of Christ*, (Omaha: IPF, 2009), 134.

5   John Paul II, *Novo Millennio Ineunte* (2001), 29.

6   Ibid., 16.

7   Josef Cardinal Ratzinger, "Taking Bearings in Christology," in *Behold the Pierced One* (San Francisco: Ignatius Press, 1984). See also Scott Hahn, "The Person and Prayer of Jesus: Reflections on the Biblical Christology of Benedict XVI" In *Spirit and Life: Interpreting the Bible in Ordinary Time* (Steubenville, OH: Emmaus Road Publishing, 2009), 11-29.

8   *Novo Millennio Ineunte*, 17-18.

9   Second Vatican Council, *Dei Verbum* (1965), 19; *Catechism of the Catholic Church* (CCC) 126, (Washington, DC: USCCB Publishing, 2000).

10   Richard Bauckham, *Jesus and the Eyewitnesses: The Gospels as Eyewitness Testimony*, (Grand Rapids: Eerdmans, 2006).

11   *Novo Millennio Ineunte*, 18.

12   Ibid., 19.

13   Ibid., 20.

14   "Taking Bearings in Christology," 26-7.

15   Ibid., 46.

16   Keating, *Resting on the Heart of Christ: The Vocation and Spirituality of the Seminary Theologian* (Omaha: IPF Publications, 2009), 135-141, 158, 161.

17   Thanks to Fr Dennis Billy for this insight into the backdrop of silence.

18   For example, Columba Marmion, *Christ in His Mysteries* (Bethesda, Md: Zaccheus Press, 2008); Bonaventure, *The Tree of Life* or the series of articles on the mysteries of the life of Jesus in *Communio* http://www.communio-icr.com/mysteries.htm.

19   See Richard Bauckham, "Jesus, Worship of," *The Anchor Bible Dictionary*, Vol. 3 (New York: Doubleday, 1992), 815.

20   John Paul II, *Novo Millennio Ineunte*, 17.

21   Richard Burridge, "About People, by People, for People: Gospel Genre and Audiences" in *The Gospel for All Christians: Rethinking the Gospel Audiences,* ed. Richard Bauckham (Grand Rapids: Eerdmans, 1998), 113-145.

22   John Paul II, *Novo Millennio Ineunte*, 28.

23   Ibid., 59.

24   John Paul II, "The Maternal Memory of the Church," in *Memory and Identity: Conversations at the Dawn of a Millennium* (New York: Rizzoli, 2005), 147-152.

25   Ratzinger, "Taking Bearings in Christology," 27-32.

26   James D. G. Dunn, *A New Perspective on Jesus: What the Quest for the Historical Jesus Missed* (Grand Rapids: Baker, 2005), 35-56; Richard Bauckham, *Jesus and the Eyewitnesses*, 240-357.

27   Philip Esler, *New Testament Theology: Communion and Commmunity* (Minneapolis: Fortress, 2005), 38-66, 229-254.

28   John Paul II, *Novo Millennio Ineunte*, 21.

29   Ratzinger, "Taking Bearings in Christology," 32-37.

30   John A McGuckin, "Mystery or Conundrum? The Apprehension of Christ in the Chalcedonian Definition" in *In the Shadow of the Incarnation*, ed. Peter Martens (Notre Dame: University of Notre Dame Press, 2008), 255-257.

31   John Paul II, *Novo Millennio Ineunte*, 23.

32   Paul VI, *Guadium et Spes* (1965), 22; John Paul II, *Redemptor Hominis* (1979), 8.

33   Ratzinger, "Bearings in Christology," 37-42.

34   International Theological Commission, "Select Questions on Christology" in *Texts and Documents 1969-1985* (San Francisco: Ignatius, 1989), 199.

35   Daniel J. Sahas, "Introduction" to *Icon and Logos: Sources in Eighth Century Iconoclasm* (University of Toronto Press, 1986), 6-8.

36   *CCC* 476-478.

37   *Novo millennio ineunte*, 25.

38   Ibid., 25-27.

39   Michael J. Gorman, *Inhabiting the Cruciform God: Kenosis, Justification and Theosis in Paul's Narrative Spirituality* (Grand Rapids: Eerdmans, 2009) Similar themes pervade the New Testament as illustrated in Larry Hurtado, "Jesus' Death as Paradigmatic in the New Testament," *Scottish Journal of Theology* 57 (2004), 413-433.

40   *Prayers and Meditations of St. Anselm with the Proslogion* translated by Benedicta Ward (New York: Penguin, 1979).

41   John Paul II, *Novo Millennio Ineunte*, 28.

42   John Paul II, *Pastores Dabo Vobis*, 72.

43   Gerald O'Collins, *Jesus A Portrait* (Maryknoll, NY: Orbis, 2008), 201-210.

Section 4

Synthesis

Contemplation and Theological Learning in Catholic Seminaries

Father Dennis J. Billy, CSsR, PhD

As I write these reflections on developing a contemplative approach to theological formation, the seminary community where I teach has just begun its annual Forty Hours Devotion. It is November 1st, the Feast of All Saints. Midterms are over. The Thanksgiving holiday is more than three weeks away. The seminarians have been given three whole days to focus on the one thing that matters most in their lives: their relationship with the Lord. The atmosphere is prayerful, yet festive. An array of flowers adorns the chapel sanctuary; the scent of incense fills the air. Although we are not officially on retreat, a heightened sense of the sacredness of time pervades our surroundings. The Liturgies are solemn; the psalms, chanted in beautiful Gregorian tones; the preaching, superb. During these days, we spend much of our time simply sitting in silence before the Blessed Sacrament. This silence permeates the air around us and draws us into a deeper relationship with the Lord. It reminds us of the contemplative foundation upon which all the rest of the program of priestly formation flows: the intellectual, the pastoral, the human, and the spiritual.

Another Kind of Devotion

As I gathered with six other theologians at Creighton University for a weekend, the image of my seminary community—seminarians, faculty, and staff—at prayer before the Blessed Sacrament was never far from my mind. Sponsored by The Institute for Priestly Formation, the seminar drew the seven of us from various points north, east, south, and west to spend time together to study the possibility of developing a contemplative approach to seminary theological formation. Our purpose was to take a few days out of our busy schedules to present papers about the way we might introduce a heightened sense of prayerfulness into our classroom pedagogy.

These days represented a devotion of a different sort because they were oriented toward the Liturgy and the Blessed Sacrament, not through the rubrics of divine worship but through the classroom. Our aim was to discuss ways in which seminary professors might help their students to integrate their academic learning with their hearts. Our reason for gathering was rooted in a simple intuition: If spiritual formation truly lay at the heart of a seminarian's theological education,[1] then seminary professors should engage not only their students' intellects, but also their souls. Seminary professors' interest in contemplative learning has its roots in this fundamental insight about the nature of theological formation. The ideas presented during our weekend together, and now gathered in this volume, are the first fruits of an ongoing reflection that we hope will continue for years to come.

Essays in Contemplative Learning

The seminar essays themselves cover a wide range of topics related to the integration of theology and spirituality in the classroom. The following summaries, while in no way exhaustive, give a good indication of the emerging paradigm resulting from our discussions. They also lay bare the intellectual and contemplative backdrop against which my own ideas on the subject have taken shape.

1. Contemplation and Vision

Deacon James Keating's paper, "Regenerating Seminary Theology: Intimacy with the Mind of Christ," offers an overarching vision of what a change in focus in seminary theological formation might be like. Instead of an overly rational approach to learning, aimed primarily at producing faithful intellectuals capable of sustained critical thinking, he envisions a curriculum where affectively imbued minds would be led to think out of prayerful silence. Such a change in focus would require seminary professors to teach their lessons out of a context of prayerfulness and pastoral charity. In doing so, they would be more conscious of the backdrop of silence from which they would teach, and they would allow that silence to enter into the rhythm of classroom learning. Such a learning theory would also help students become vulnerable to truth and to intimacy with Christ and allow them to integrate the learning of their minds with the yearning of their hearts.

Deacon Keating claims that this change in focus would help overcome the ongoing split between spirituality and theology, between affective maturity and critical thinking, and between a hermeneutics of trust and a hermeneutics of suspicion. The seminary classroom, he asserts, is one of the primary places where students of theology can be encouraged to "think in prayer" and to "pray in their thinking." He maintains that dialogue between spiritual directors and seminary professors would be a helpful starting point for paving the way for the integration of contemplation and theological learning. As a helpful tool for implementing such learning, he identifies a "double-entry" system of classroom note-taking, whereby students would record both theological concepts and their affective responses to those concepts.

2. Learning and Virtue

In his paper "The Love of Learning in the Life of the Diocesan Priest," Father Thomas McDermott, OP, stresses the importance of seminarians developing a habit of lifelong learning. The paper acknowledges the great difficulty of doing so in the midst of a material and cultural nihilism that considers life meaningless and views study and the quest of knowledge as ultimately pointless. At the same time, it recognizes that one of the signs of a living love of God is a desire for the divine fueled by a sacred curiosity of the faith that leads to joy. This virtue of sacred learning gives the seminarian and future priest a transforming knowledge that carries him to the threshold of the sacred.

Father McDermott identifies five factors that mitigate against seminarians fostering a habit of lifelong learning: (1) the difficulty of attaining genuine spiritual growth, (2) defective knowledge, (3) the constant noise of life, (4) shallow activism, and (5) an excessive trust in oneself. He also states that the lack of forming a habit of lifelong learning may be one of the underlying causes of burnout in the life of a diocesan priest.

By way of negative example, the factors that block a habit of lifelong learning point to the underlying positive factors involved in nurturing such a habit: perseverance, dedication to the truth, solitude, prayerful action, and trust in God. The seminary professor needs to find concrete ways to minimize the negative factors and to enhance the positive factors. The paper plants the seeds of a genuine spirituality of contemplative learning that will enable diocesan priests to be devout yet learned men of God who are open to the promptings of the Spirit in their lives and dedicated to the well-being of the people whom they serve.

3. Prayer as Leaven

Father Thomas Lane's paper, "Scripture and Prayer: A Fuller Methodology," examines the relationship between prayer and the various methodologies used in the study of Scripture. He roots his reflections in the *Program of Priestly Formation*, sections 199-200, which emphasizes the need of the historical-critical method for sound exegesis, as well as other critical methods that can be used to discover the depth and richness of the divinely inspired texts. He cites numerous papal and magisterial documents which applaud the used of such methods in the proper interpretation of God's Word. Simultaneously, he uses those same documents to point out that teaching Scripture in the seminary has the primarily pastoral end of helping the faithful interpret the meaning of God's Word for their lives.

Father Lane is quick to point out the limitations of the historical-critical method of interpretation and recognizes the need of all students of the Scripture to be aware of the philosophical underpinnings of whatever method they are using to interpret it. His analysis points to the need to recognize a broader basis of rationality from which those who study God's Word can integrate its insights with the depth of vision that comes through a mutual dialogue between faith and reason. For this reason, he recognizes the need to purify the historical-critical method of its narrow understanding of rationality and the need be able to interpret the sacred text with the mind of Christ. His paper also brings to the surface a need for an approach to interpreting the Scriptures that addresses *all* the dimensions of human existence, not the intellectual alone. In this respect, his paper does not view prayer in opposition to the historical-critical method but as a transforming leaven that may actually be that method's salvation.

4. A Patristic Model

Dr. Perry Cahall's paper, "Lecture *Divina*: The Fathers of the Church and Theological Pedagogy," offers a sapiential approach to seminary theological formation. It focuses on the centrality of love in the mind of the Church Fathers and looks to them as models of what it means to be contemplative teachers of theology. Dr. Cahall draws an analogy from the *lectio divina*, the contemplative reading of a text, and says that the dynamics of a seminary theology class should be more a "lecture" *divina*, a meditative presentation and listening to the wisdom of the Church's living tradition, rather than a mere academic exercise focusing on a rational presentation of abstract theories. He identifies five characteristics of the theology of the Church Fathers applicable to a contemplative approach to seminary theological education. The contemplative theologian, in his mind, should focus on: (1) the centrality of love, (2) presenting theology as more than an intellectual exercise, (3) relating everything to Jesus, (4) thinking with the Church, and (5) giving witness to the faith. These qualities, which touched the very heart of the patristic era and continued in the integrated love of learning and desire for God that characterized the theology of the monastic schools, need to be retrieved by today's theological seminaries.

According to Dr. Cahall, the People of God have need of learned saints who desire to lead others to God, who view the study of theology as a way of entering more deeply into the divine, who understand that reason cannot be separated from Jesus, the Word-made-flesh, who view faithfulness, not originality, as the mark of a good theologian, and who teach, first and foremost, by the witness of their lives. He believes that the seminary theology professor should espouse such ideals and find concrete ways to manifest them in his or her classroom pedagogy.

5. A Contemplative Lecture

Dr. Margaret Turek's paper, "Balthasar's Approach to a Theology of God the Father: Theology at the Service of Spirituality," offers an extended meditation on the Fatherhood of God in the thought of Hans Urs von Balthasar. It integrates theology and prayer and represents a fine example of what a classroom lecture rooted in a contemplative approach to theological learning might look like. It also gives the reader a rare glimpse into the developing classroom genre of "lecture" *divina*, a form of classroom presentation which incorporates prayer, meditative reading, and silence into an integrating intellectual and affective learning experience.

Dr. Turek identifies the modern "God Problem" rooted in a false human/Divine dichotomy, which pits humanity's impotence against an omnipotent God. She uses Balthasar's theology of the Father to deflate this false dichotomy by showing that God's omnipotence manifests itself in powerlessness, vulnerability, and weakness. She further asserts that Jesus' intimate relationship with the Father reveals the true focus of the Divine-human relationship. Rather than imagining an omnipotent God rendering humanity omnipotent, she envisions Divine omnipotence empowering humanity through powerlessness. From these insights, she draws out a number of important ramifications for the spiritual fatherhood of the priesthood that have implications for the development of a contemplative pedagogy for seminary theological formation. Dr. Turek's paper provides an excellent example of how such a contemplative approach to learning can be used as a way to integrate spirituality and theology in the classroom experience.

6. Contemplating the Face of Christ

Dr. John Gresham's paper, "Contemplating Christ in the Classroom," examines what a course in Christology would look like if it focused specifically on the primary goal of seminary training: bringing students into intimacy with Christ. Inspired by John Paul II's emphasis on the importance of believers contemplating the face of Christ,[2] the paper envisions what an entire course in Christology might look like if professor and students alike contemplated the ideas conveyed in the classroom in such a way that the ideas functioned as channels of spiritual growth and led the professor and students to a deeper experience of God. The discipline of Christology, it maintains, touches the very heart of seminary formation, since its subject matter focuses specifically on knowledge of Christ and union with Him.

Dr. Gresham offers a serious analysis of what a contemplative approach to learning would mean for this discipline. He emphasizes the doxological origins of doctrine (*lex orandi, lex credendi*) and demonstrates how worship gives birth to doctrine and finds its completion in action (*lex agendi*). He also suggests a number of practical pedagogical techniques that professors can use to create an atmosphere of contemplative learning in the classroom. If it is true that contemplation (*contemplatio*) leads to communion (*communio*), and ultimately to mission (*missio*), then it follows that a course in Christology dedicated to contemplating the face of Christ through an extended reflection upon the doctrinal formulations of the Church should lead to both a deeper intimacy with Christ and a heightened sense of the Christian's call to purposeful action in the world.

Taken together, these seminar papers offer the first glimpse of a fundamental paradigm shift taking place in seminary theological formation. Rather than being wed to a narrow scientific model of rational inquiry into the truths of the faith, this emerging contemplative pedagogy seeks to integrate reason and faith, mind and heart, spirituality and theology into a new approach to theological learning that addresses every dimension of human existence.

Emerging Challenges

When discussing these papers on a contemplative approach to seminary theological education, a number of issues arose which called for further reflection and which may well be the subject of future gatherings. As reflection on the emerging shift in paradigms in seminary education continues, the theological community must face these issues head-on so that the level of discourse may continue to be of help to the professor's classroom pedagogy. What follows are three useful suggestions about the needs of the contemplative paradigm and its future development.

1. The Need for a Consistent Vocabulary

An emerging field of inquiry within a particular discipline must address new needs and concepts in a way that is recognizable by those within the discipline. It must also be aware that the vocabulary it uses may be weighed down by baggage associated with past usage. One of the challenges in the field of contemplative pedagogy is to employ a consistent vocabulary that is both easily recognizable and clearly delineated and unique in its usage.

During the seminar, it soon became obvious that a common vocabulary would help to avoid confusion and assist in developing a contemplative approach to learning. The use of terms such as "method" and "pedagogy," for example, stems from theology's association with the empirical and social sciences and might give the false impression that the acquisition of wisdom can be packaged into a "ready-made" recipe. Terms such as "way" and "manner" are more preferable, since they coincide with an understanding of contemplation as, "a gift freely bestowed which draws a person through the attraction of divine grace."

Throughout the discussion, moreover, the term "contemplation," itself, was used in a vague and, at best, very general sense. Such usage was very different from the classic understanding of a wordless, mystical state of awareness brought on entirely by the movement of the Holy Spirit in one's life and distinguished from the more discursive and affective form of Christian prayer known as "meditation." While a preference for the term "contemplation" is understandable (and not without merit), the larger, more fluid sense in which it was being used needs to be emphasized, as well as its marked affinities with the Christian meditation. As used by the presenters, "contemplation" is "meditative" in that it involves reflecting upon the mysteries of the faith with both mind and heart against a backdrop of silence, and "mystical" in that it helps a person to live the Gospel on ever deeper levels of consciousness.

Finally, the contemplative approach needs to be very clear about the particular type of theology it is seeking to foster. If, in the past, seminary theological formation relied on the insights of scholasticism's use of dialectic and syllogistic reasoning and, perhaps more recently, on theology's attempt to pattern itself after the empirical sciences, the contemplative approach, while not denying the important insights of these approaches to the faith, is more interested in the acquisition of theological wisdom. In this respect, it has more in common with the sapiential approach of monastic theology's *lectio divina* than scholasticism's attempt to identify the objective truths of the faith or modern theology's fascination with the historical-critical method. By clarifying its understanding of the nature of theology as "faith seeking understanding" (*fides quaerens intellectum*), it will avoid confusion with other legitimate models of theological inquiry and have a better chance gaining a sympathetic hearing in the forum of theological exchange.

2. Developing a Theological Anthropology

A contemplative approach to seminary theological formation also needs to be rooted in a sound theological anthropology, one which takes into account all of the dimensions of human existence. St. Paul's tripartite body/soul/spirit anthropology (1 Thes 5:23) when coupled with the social and transcendental dimensions of his doctrine of the body of Christ (1 Cor 12:12-13) provides a good Scriptural foundation that will help students to be vulnerable to the truth about themselves and their relationship to God.

Rooted in the insights of Sacred Scripture, the contemplative approach seeks to address *all* of the dimensions of humanity's anthropological makeup: the physical, the psychological, the intellectual, the spiritual, and the social. Professors who employ it seek to educate the whole person, not just the mind. For this reason, they need to strike a balance between a critical analysis of ideas and an affective assimilation of them. Because theology for them is as much an art as it is a science, they recognize the value of allowing the silent backdrop against which they teach to come to the fore at appropriate moments to heighten their vulnerability to truth. They are also aware that the contemplative approach has at least three levels of learning: the experiential, the doctrinal, and the analytical.[3] While seminary theological formation has generally focused primarily on the latter two, the contemplative approach seeks to address all three levels, but with particular emphasis on the experiential.

Finally, a sound theological anthropology will enable seminary professors to be aware of the many ways in which their teaching affects their students. They will be conscious that the presentation of their material touches their students on the level of body, soul, and spirit not only as individuals, but also as a group. For this reason, they will encourage their classes to engage the material presented to them as a

community of learning. Professors using this approach understand all too well that group dynamics within a class can
have a strong effect on the way the individuals, themselves,
assimilate material. For this reason, professors using this approach will generally seek out and implement specific tools
to address the effects of group learning on individuals—and
vice versa.

3. Drawing Connections

Because of its sapiential understanding of theology,
the contemplative approach shares certain characteristics
with Christian meditation and spiritual direction. When
the contemplative approach is applied to the classroom, the
underlying structure of these venerable practices provides a
welcomed point of continuity in the seminarian's experience
of prayer, direction, and theological learning.

a. Christian Meditation

As the soul's intimate conversation with God, Christian meditation takes place against a backdrop of silence and
typically contains a period of preparation, the meditative
body or corpus, and a conclusion. The preparation normally
includes a brief act of faith ("Lord, I believe in you"), an act
of humility ("Lord, have mercy on me"), and a request for
guidance ("Lord, give me light"). The body of the meditation
typically has four moments: (1) a reflection on a particular
facet of the faith, (2) an affective response to the reflection,

usually in the form of a heartfelt prayer to God, (3) a presentation of one's needs to God in the form of a petition, and (4) a response to the previous steps in the form of a practical resolution that will deepen one's relationship with God. The conclusion usually consists of a time for giving thanks ("Lord, thank you for the light I have received"), a request for help ("Lord, help me to carry out my resolution"), and a brief prayer for perseverance ("Lord, help me to remain forever faithful to you"). All of these moments take place against a backdrop of silence or solitude of heart, which allows the heart to listen to the movement of the Spirit and to enter into prayerful dialogue with it.[4]

b. Spiritual Direction

These dynamics of meditation can easily be projected onto the plane of spiritual direction. A typical session, for example, can begin with a brief period silence, during which time the director and directee together make a brief act of faith in God, an act of humility, and a request for light. As they enter into the body of the session, the director invites the directee to reflect on the events of his or her life since the last session (reflection), assists the directee in getting in touch with his or her feelings about what has been shared (affection), helps the directee to identify his or her different needs regarding what has been shared (petition), and encourages the directee to decide upon a practical and concrete course of action (resolution). As with meditation, all of these steps take place against a backdrop of silence and solitude of heart so that the directee can listen to his or her heart and

162 of 180 of 180

discern what the Lord is saying. As with meditation, the session draws to a close with another period of silence where both the director and directee thank God for the guidance given, ask for the grace to perform the decided upon course of action, and also pray for the grace of perseverance.[5]

c. Theological Learning

These same dynamics that are so characteristic of meditation and spiritual direction are also common to the contemplative approach to theological formation. The class begins in silent prayer, where professor and students alike make an act of faith, an act of humility, and a request for light. As the class gets underway, this silence recedes as a backdrop against which the presentation of the material and the discussion can take place. The professor presents the topic for the day using a variety of means to get his point across (reflection), assists the students to get in touch with their affective response to the material presented (affection), enables them to bring to the surface the various needs raised by the material (petition), and helps them to formulate a specific course of action to take as a result of such learning (resolution). During this time, the professor is careful to allow the backdrop of silence to come to the fore so that the students can avert to the presence of the Spirit in their lives as a silent third party. The classroom session ends with an appropriate period of silence, where those present thank God for what they have learned, ask for the strength to do what they agreed needed to be done, and make a specific request for the grace of perseverance.

To facilitate a contemplative approach to learning, students should be encouraged to take notes in a double-entry format by recording the content of the lesson presented to them one side of a page and their affective response, needs, and practical decisions regarding it on another side. In doing so, they will be better able to integrate the intellectual content presented to them with other important dimensions of their lives. Because the dynamics of their classroom learning resemble those that go on in the conversations that they have with God and with their spiritual directors, they have a better chance of drawing important connections between what goes on in the classroom and other important areas of their lives.

Conclusion

As I complete this essay, the Forty Hours Devotion at my seminary has long since passed. Classes have resumed, and the seminary community has returned to its normal routine. If, on the surface, nothing much seems to have changed, beneath it, the Spirit continues to touch our hearts and to shape us in small, seemingly insignificant ways. The memory of that precious time of quiet prayer before the Blessed Sacrament lingers as a gentle reminder of the reason why we exist and do what we do here at the seminary. It also represents a call to simplify our lives and to dedicate ourselves even further to living the Gospel on ever deeper levels of awareness: even when in the classroom.

As I look back with fond memories on the time I spent with my six colleagues some months ago, I see with more clarity than ever the importance of the task we set out to accomplish. Our time together was a devotion to the Lord of a different, but no less important, kind. Built on the intuition that there are important contemplative dimensions to the learning process that need to be tapped into and brought to the surface of the seminary classroom, the approach we have taken seeks to demonstrate how spiritual formation plays a central and truly integrating role in the life of a seminary community.

Although we recognize that we are only at the beginning of developing a contemplative approach to theological learning suitable for the seminary classroom, we are encouraged by the progress that we have made in so short a time and by the direction our prayer, reflections, and sharing are taking us. Our sincere hope is that the approach to theological learning proposed in this book will take root in Catholic seminaries here, in the United States, and throughout the world. We believe that doing so will help to insure that the priests of tomorrow will be holy and learned men equipped with the pastoral wisdom needed to lead the people whom they serve along the way of holiness.

Notes

1   United States Conference of Catholic Bishops, *Program of Priestly Formation*, 5ᵗʰ ed. (Washington, DC: USCCB, 2006), 115.

2   John Paul II, *Novo Millennio Ineunte* (2001), 16.

3   This distinction is adapted from Walter Principe's, "Toward Defining Spirituality," *Sciences Religieuses/Studies in Religion* 12/2 (1983): 135-37.

4   This manner of Christian meditation comes from St. Alphonsus de Liguori and is presented in popular form for today's readers in Dennis Billy, *Plentiful Redemption: An Introduction to Alphonsian Spirituality* (Liguori, MO: Liguori Publications, 2001), 21-37. For a more detailed presentation of Alphonsus' teaching, see Alphonsus de Liguori, *Mental Prayer*, in *The Complete Works of Saint Alphonsus de Liguori*, ed. Eugene Grimm, vol. 3 (Brooklyn, St. Louis, Toronto: Redemptorist Fathers, 1927), 252-284. This treatise is a compilation of different extracts from Alphonsus' writings, the largest part of which comes from chapter 15 of *The True Spouse of Jesus Christ*.

5   For the application of this model of Christian meditation to the dynamics of spiritual direction, see Dennis J. Billy, "An Alphonsian Model of Spiritual Direction," *Studia moralia* 41(2003): 47-72; Idem, With Open Heart: Spiritual Direction in the Alphonsian Tradition (Liguori, MO: Liguori Publications, 2003), 65-80.

CPSIA information can be obtained at www.ICGtesting.com
Printed in the USA
LVOW080751150213

320227LV00001B/2/P